Your Prenatal Eclipse

Rose Lineman

First Printing: 1992
Current Printing: 2003
ISBN Number: 0-86690-415-8
Library of Congress Catalog Number: 92-81324

Cover design: Christel Bonnett

Published by:
American Federation of Astrologers, Inc.
6535 S. Rural Road
Tempe, Arizona 85283

Printed in the United States of America

Dedication

To my parents who brought me into this world, love, nurtured and encouraged me—until we meet again.

Other books by Rose Lineman

Compendium of Astrology (with Jan Popelka)
Eclipses: Astrological Guideposts
Eclipse Interpretation Manual

Acknowledgments

I am deeply grateful to Robbie Leckie and
Lynn Ray for help with research and technical assistance,
and to Cary Franks who initially sparked the interest in
eclipses that led to this book and two others in the series.
Thank you.

Contents

List of Illustrations

List of Tables

Introduction

One's prenatal eclipse, the last solar eclipse to occur prior to birth, does more than initiate the continuous cycle of eclipses a person experiences during a lifetime. It reveals, in part, the karma one has built up in prior incarnations; it discloses karmic relationships and situations with which one must deal in order to gain karmic progress, and it points out avenues through which one can work out karmic problems.

Although the prenatal eclipse does not progress as natal planets do, it is continually reactivated throughout one's lifetime by progressed planets and major transits which aspect it. It is when progressed and transiting aspects to one's prenatal eclipse form that people with whom one shares karmic ties enter their lives, that karmic situations arise, that one encounters *deja vu* experiences.

This book explores karmic implications of the prenatal eclipse, the key planet and other related factors. The prenatal eclipse summarizes those parts of all prior incarnations relevant to the current lifetime and describes certain aspects of one's progress, or lack of it, on the evolutionary wheel. The key planet, the natal planet that lies directly ahead of the prenatal eclipse in the zodiac (counterclockwise in the horoscope) with no planets between (nodes or angles are not considered here), yields information about the immediately prior incarnation and facts about the transition which ended that particular life cycle. It describes developments that took place during the most recent past life which have karmic bearing upon the present life.

This book presents astrological techniques that enable one to identify karmic responsibilities and determine appropriate ways to fulfill those responsibilities. It describes prenatal eclipse indications that point out personal attitudes and characteristics to be cultivated in order to develop a positive approach to karmic problems. The use of comparison charts to assess karmic relationships, major eclipse periods in life, the significance of the initial eclipse in the Saros series to which the prenatal eclipse belongs, and motivations common to the numbers of people who share the same prenatal eclipse are among numerous topics discussed in this book. Detailed interpretations of the karmic significance of the sign and house occupied by the prenatal eclipse and of the aspects it forms are included along with example charts.

It is through study of the prenatal eclipse and the astrological elements with which it is associated that one can begin to unravel the mysteries of past lives and find meaning in the present.

Chapter 1

Your Prenatal Eclipse: A Beginning

Your prenatal eclipse is the hallmark of a new beginning, a rebirth in the cycle of reincarnation. It reveals much about the inner nature and maps a path to spiritual understanding and development. It also explains relationships; it identifies perplexing situations and problems and points to ways to resolve them. The key planet, the initial eclipse of the Saros series to which your prenatal eclipse belongs, and the lunar eclipse(s) that appear in sequence with your prenatal eclipse add depth to astrological interpretation and karmic understanding.

Charting Procedures

To determine the position of your prenatal eclipse, find in the eclipse table in the Appendix the last solar eclipse to appear prior to the time of birth. This is your prenatal eclipse. Do not use a lunar eclipse as the prenatal eclipse even if it occurred closer to the birthdate than the last solar eclipse. Usually, the date of the prenatal eclipse does not coincide with the birthdate, but it can, especially for those individuals who make a last-minute decision to reenter the earth plane. If a solar eclipse occurs on the birthdate, the time at which it began is of

Table 1		*Initial Eclipses for Saros Series*

Series Number	North Node Series	South Node Series
1	13♑	29♌-00♍
2-E*	6♋ (ends 8/3/2024)	---
2	26♊ (began 6/17/1928)	2♉
3	22♎	27♌
4	11♊	27♈
5-E*	---	Unknown (ended 9/12/31)
5	19♎	22♋ (began 7/14/1784)
6	28♉	22♓
7	17♎	7♋
8	6♊	11♈
9-E*	17♌ (ended 1/5/1935)	5♋ (ended 7/22/1971)
9	28♌ (began 8/21/1664)	26♋ (began 7/19/1917)
10	10♉	26♓
11	16♌	29♊-0♋
12-E*	---	6♎ (ended 4/8/2002)
12	28♉	23♒ (began 2/12/1812)
13	21♌	6♊
14	15♉	10♍
15	27♋	24♊
16	6♓	28♍
17-E*	12♋ (ended 8/12/1942)	---
17	5♌ (began 7/28/1870)	11♊
18	21♒	3♍
19	21♋	Unknown

*The earlier starting of two concurrently operating members of the same series.

utmost importance. A solar eclipse that begins prior to the moment of birth, even by seconds, is the prenatal eclipse although it does not reach maximum obscuration until after birth. A solar eclipse that begins after the very moment of birth is not the prenatal eclipse. Though it may have much impact on the natal chart, it has no karmic significance unless associated factors indicate otherwise. Regardless of whether your prenatal eclipse occurs six months before or within moments of birth or any time between, its astrological aftereffect and karmic message are imprinted upon the horoscope.

When you find your prenatal eclipse in the eclipse table, note its zodiacal position, the node at which it occurred (N==north, S=south), type (total, annular or partial) and its geographical longitude and latitude at the time it began at the noon point, or in the case of a partial eclipse, the greatest eclipse point, and its location at the time it ended. Find the lunar eclipse that accompanied the prenatal eclipse and note its zodiacal position and type (total, partial or appulse). An accompanying lunar eclipse will have the same Saros series number as the prenatal eclipse but will occur at the opposite Node. It will appear approximately two weeks before or after the prenatal eclipse event, and can occur after birth. In some instances, two accompanying lunar eclipses occur, one prior to and the other following the appearance of the prenatal eclipse. In this case, record data for both lunar eclipses.

Also note the Saros series number of the prenatal eclipse and find the zodiacal position of its initial eclipse in Table 1. Initial eclipses listed apply only to solar eclipses; initial eclipses of lunar series are unknown.

Enter your prenatal eclipse (PE), its accompanying lunar eclipse (LE) and initial eclipse (IE) in your natal horoscope as you would a planet. On the chart form, list the prenatal eclipses' geographical longitudes and latitudes shown in the table in the Appendix.

For example, the eclipse table shows that the prenatal eclipse for a male born April 23, 1978 occurred April 7 of that year, 16 days before birth. A partial South Node eclipse, its zodiacal position is 17 Aries 27, and it belongs to Saros series 16S, whose initial eclipse is shown to be 28 Virgo in Table 1. The prenatal eclipse was preceded on March 24 by a total lunar

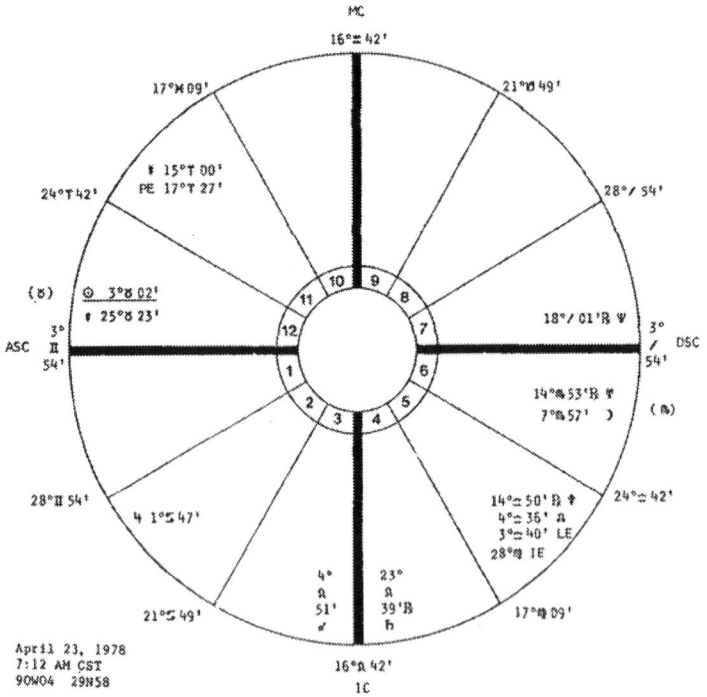

Figure 1   Paul's Natal Horoscope

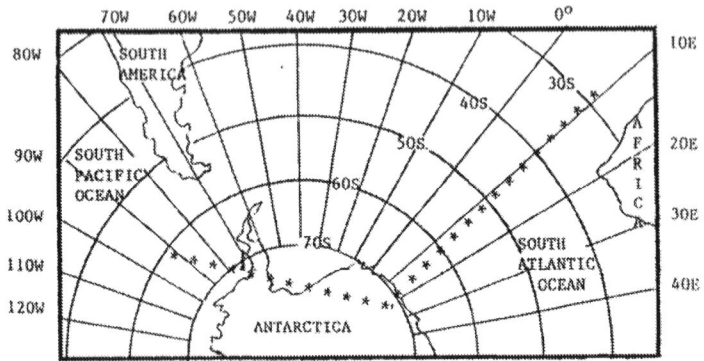

Figure 2   Paul's Prenatal Eclipse Line

4

eclipse (16N series) at 3 Libra 40. Note how these positions are entered in Figure 1.

The prenatal eclipse is in the natal eleventh house; the accompanying lunar eclipse and initial eclipse are in the fifth. The geographical location of the prenatal eclipse at the beginning point to the nearest degree is 92W/62S; at the greatest eclipse point it is 23E/72S; it ends at 10E/29S. A line drawn on a geographical map that starts at the beginning point, passes through the greatest eclipse point (or noon point for total and annular eclipses) and ends at the ending point is called the prenatal eclipse line, and is significant to interpretation. It is an esoteric symbol representative of past life geographical contact (Figure 2).

For a male born July 19, 1980, the prenatal eclipse, which was total, occurred near the South Node several months earlier than birth, on February 16. It appeared in 26 Aquarius 50. The initial eclipse of Saros series 18S to which this prenatal eclipse belongs falls in 3 Virgo. The prenatal eclipse was followed on March 1 by a lunar appulse (penumbral eclipse) of the 18N series that appeared in 11 Virgo 26. The prenatal eclipse line extends from 15W/1S, passes through 49E/1N and ends at 108E/27N (see Figures 3 and 4).

After entering your prenatal eclipse, its accompanying lunar eclipse(s) and the initial eclipse in the natal horoscope, aspect them, using natal orbs for your prenatal eclipse and two degrees for the initial eclipse and accompanying lunar eclipse. Determine your prenatal eclipse line.

Next, locate the key planet in the natal horoscope and circle it, underline or otherwise indicate its importance in the chart. This is the natal planet that lies directly ahead of the prenatal eclipse in the natural order of the zodiac, counterclockwise in the chart, with no planets separating them. Nodes, angles or other sensitive points are not relevant here and cannot be con-

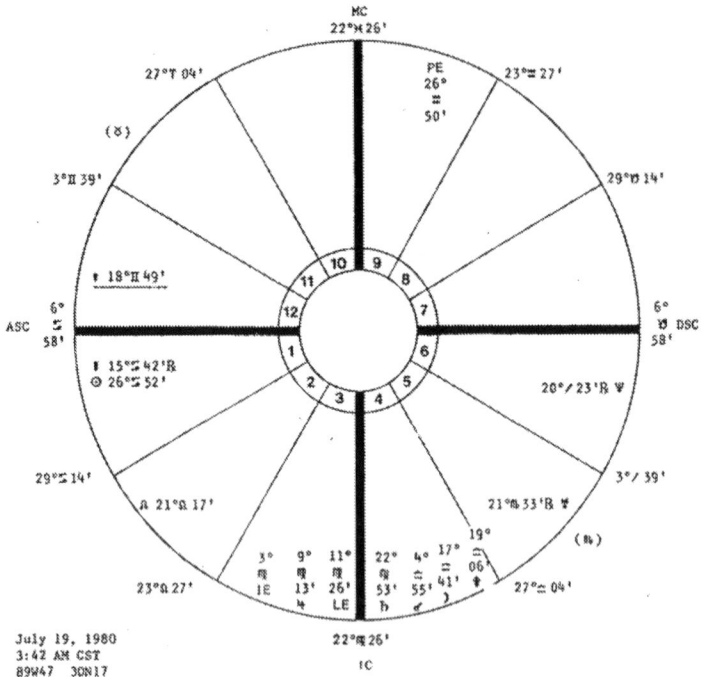

Figure 3   Martin's Natal Horoscope

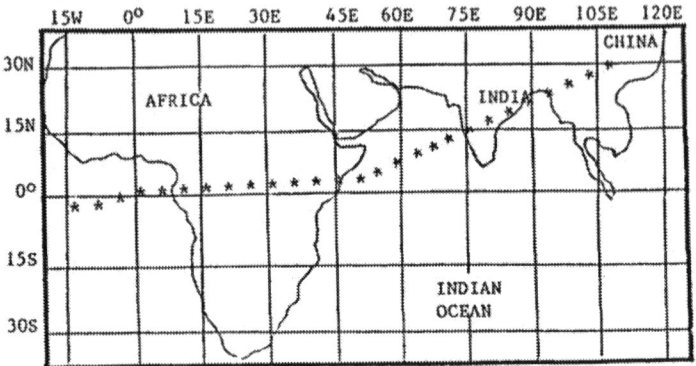

Figure 4   Martin's Prenatal Eclipse Line

6

sidered key points in relation to the prenatal eclipse. In a sense, the prenatal eclipse always "leads" the key planet, for if the prenatal eclipse were an actual planet, it would always rise immediately before the key planet clockwise in the chart.

In Figure 1, the key planet is the Sun, posited in 3 Taurus 02, a distance of 15 degrees 35 minutes ahead of the prenatal eclipse counterclockwise in the chart.

The key planet in Figure 3 is Venus in 18 Gemini 49. In this example, the prenatal eclipse and key planet are separated by 111 degrees and 59 minutes.

List the aspects the key planet forms in your natal chart and add any aspects it forms with the prenatal eclipse, accompanying lunar eclipse(s) or the initial eclipse. Calculate the zodiacal distance that separates the key planet from the prenatal eclipse.

Summary

Before you study the karmic factors in your chart represented by the prenatal eclipse, the accompanying lunar eclipse(s), the initial eclipse and the key planet, proceed as follows:

1. Enter your prenatal eclipse in your natal horoscope and aspect. Note its type and the Node involved; record its geographical position at the beginning point, noon/greatest point and ending point.

2. Draw your prenatal eclipse line on a world map, connecting the coordinates listed in Step 1.

3. Enter the accompanying lunar eclipse(s) in your natal horoscope and aspect. Note its type and whether it occurred prior to or following your prenatal eclipse.

4. Enter the initial eclipse in your natal horoscope and aspect. Include an aspect with the prenatal eclipse and accompanying lunar eclipse(s) if any exist.

5. Locate your key planet. Calculate the zodiacal distance

that separates it from your prenatal eclipse; record.

6. Note all natal aspects to the key planet and those it forms with the prenatal eclipse, the accompanying lunar eclipse and the initial eclipse.

At this point you have the basic data you need to begin interpretation.

Chapter 2

The Past, Present and Future

From an esoteric point of view, the past cannot be isolated from the present because we are the sum total of our past. The present cannot be separated from the future, for what we are now is part of what we will become.

The prenatal eclipse and the astrological elements with which it is associated give information about past lives, rebirth, situations and relationships encountered during the present lifetime and point to directions that enable us, in a sense, to control our future in terms of karmic progress.

Each karmic factor plays a different yet significant role in interpretation. Interpretational orientation and emphasis vary. These factors compare to the pieces of a puzzle. The picture is not complete until all the pieces, large and small, have been placed as they properly fit. Upon analysis of the prenatal eclipse and associated elements—initial eclipse, accompanying lunar eclipse and key planet—and integration of the resultant astrological facts, a karmic portrait emerges. The choice to follow or not the course described therein is up to the individual, but the path to karmic progress is clearly indicated.

Prenatal Eclipse
Interpretational Guidelines

The prenatal eclipse is the primary significator in determining one's karmic path. It is associated with any or all prior lifetimes and deals specifically with karmic debts or assets that pertain to the present. How one responds to the message of the prenatal eclipse forms the foundation for the future.

The sign position of the prenatal eclipse, though common to large numbers of individuals born between two consecutive solar eclipses, has a particular orientation in each individual chart. Interpretation of the prenatal eclipse in each of the signs and general sign influence is given in Chapter 3.

The house position of the prenatal eclipse describes affairs, situations and relationships through which karmic lessons can be recognized and, hopefully, dealt with in a manner productive of karmic progress. This house is extremely important, and is viewed as an avenue of karmic resource, not as a problem area. Its interests are assets to be utilized in resolving karmic debts. Interpretation of the prenatal eclipse in each of the houses is discussed in detail in Chapter 4.

Aspects the prenatal eclipse forms within the natal chart give direction to the potentials described by its sign and house position and point to specific problems (hard aspects) and the means of resolving problems (easy aspects) according to the natures of the planets involved, their sign and house positions, and their emphasis in the horoscope. Chapter 5 is devoted to explicit meanings of prenatal eclipses and natal aspects.

Aspects formed by progressed or transiting planets to the prenatal eclipse act as triggering mechanisms which activate dormant potentials associated with the prenatal eclipse and related factors according to the nature of the aspecting planet, its sign and house position, and the type of aspect. Exact hard progressed and transiting aspects are associated with actual events. Easy aspects depict circumstances, conditions or relationships that assist one in overcoming karmic barriers. Such aspects are interpreted in Chapter 6.

The promise of the prenatal eclipse does not end with the individual horoscope. Although the prenatal eclipse may point to general relationships, it is only through an aspect between one person's prenatal eclipse and the horoscope of another person that the actual relationship and its meaning on an esoteric plane can be identified. The various types of prenatal eclipse ties and karmic relationships are covered in Chapter 7.

In addition to sign and house position of the prenatal eclipse and the aspects it forms, one must consider the prenatal eclipse line. This is the line that extends from the geographic prenatal eclipse beginning point, through the noon/greatest point to the ending point. The way to determine and draw this line is given in Chapter 1. After having drawn the line on a world map, extend the coordinates by five degrees north, south, east and west to form a perimeter enclosing the prenatal eclipse line. The enclosed area outlines a part of earth that had meaning in past lives. It may include a place where you were born at one time, lived or died. When the prenatal eclipse line crosses a particular country or city, you can be certain that you were there some time in history, and it may indicate a former nationality. Lines that are placed entirely within bodies of water suggest an innate interest in the sea, perhaps death from drowning, or the existence of an island long gone from the face of the earth, a place that played a major part in your past. In the event the prenatal eclipse line lies within uninhabited polar regions, it is more difficult to interpret. However, this line must be viewed in context with other karmic factors. For example, Figure 2 in Chapter 1 shows that Paul's prenatal eclipse line lies almost entirely within the South Pacific and South Atlantic Oceans, crossing points near the coast of Antarctica and apparently missing the western coast of South Africa. With his prenatal eclipse in Aries conjunct Mercury, trine Saturn, inconjunct Uranus, trine Neptune and opposing Pluto, we may have an early seafarer here or only one who dreamed adventurous dreams ahead of his time. Complete analysis of the horoscope may yield further dues to this part of his past.

Figure 4 shows that Martin's prenatal eclipse line crosses Africa, southern India, northern Burma and extends into southern China. His past relates in some way to each of these ancient lands, perhaps at different times.

If any point in your prenatal eclipse line, including the extended enclosed area, touches or crosses the prenatal eclipse line area of another person, an intersection of past lives is indicated. You know where former contact between the two of you took place, though this geographical coincidence does not tell you when.

The type of solar eclipse that occurs as your prenatal eclipse also bears upon interpretation. A total eclipse indicates that one must work harder to take advantage of prenatal eclipse resources. One must take the initiative to open up resource areas depicted in the horoscope in order to utilize them fully. An annular eclipse, with its brilliant corona, may not open the door, but it creates an inborn awareness that enables one to more readily recognize the manner in which to best utilize karmic assets. A partial eclipse eases the path in the sense that the affairs, situations and relationships considered karmic assets are not only apparent to the individual but are also easily accessible.

Consider also the position of the prenatal eclipse relative to the Moon's Nodes. An eclipse that occurs near the North Node suggests that the individual has reached a point in evolvement where he or she is not bound by inborn biases or negative attitudes which may have stalled karmic progress in the past. This

12

person finds it comparatively easy to reach out in the earth plane to avenues of spiritual enlightenment. A South Node prenatal eclipse is indicative of strongly entrenched innate prejudices or negative habits acquired over several past lives which preclude spiritual growth. It is essential that the individual overcome these inner barriers before the first step can be taken to resolve karmic issues shown in the horoscope.

When analyzing the prenatal eclipse, consider the influence its dispositor (the planetary ruler of the sign it occupies) exercises in the horoscope. Keep in mind that each planet, sign and house have various attributes. When examining the prenatal eclipse and associated factors, findings must be carefully sifted to determine how they apply to a particular natal horoscope.

Significance of the Initial Eclipse

As the common progenitor of all eclipses belonging to the same Saros series as the prenatal eclipse, the initial eclipse, through its sign and house positions and aspects, links the prenatal eclipse to astrological elements with which the prenatal eclipse may not be directly associated. It serves, in effect, as a relay factor, and as such broadens the scope of prenatal eclipse interpretation. Its sign expression colors that of the prenatal eclipse and its house position ties in activities of that house to those of the house occupied by the prenatal eclipse.

Sign qualities of the initial eclipse delicately shade prenatal eclipse sign expression much as the ascending sign colors to a degree the entire horoscope. To interpret, evaluate sign attributes of both eclipses. View the sign of the initial eclipse as one through which the sign of the prenatal eclipse functions. Look for similarities and contrasts in natural sign expression. The main emphasis is on the sign of the prenatal eclipse; the sign of the initial eclipse adds to prenatal eclipse sign qualities a flavor not seen in pure sign expression. Sign influence of the initial eclipse, although always subtle, becomes more pronounced when the prenatal eclipse occupies a sign of the same triplicity or in a duad of another sign that shares similar characteristics. In these instances, initial eclipse sign qualities reinforce prenatal eclipse sign expression. Even though signs may not be compatible, sub-rulers may help bring out positive aspects of both signs. For example, although Paul's initial and prenatal eclipses are inconjunct by sign (Figure 1), his initial eclipse is in the Taurus (Venus) decan and Leo (Sun) duad of Virgo, ruled by Mercury. His prenatal eclipse is in the Leo (Sun) decan and Libra (Venus) duad of Aries, ruled by Mars, so he has Sun and Venus qualities from both eclipses upon which to draw; Sun qualities that compliment Mars and Venus attributes that soften abrasiveness. Each known initial eclipse and its general influence on eclipses following in the series are interpreted in my *Eclipse Interpretation Manual.*

The house in which the initial eclipse falls acts as an auxiliary to the house of the prenatal eclipse. Whereas the house of the prenatal eclipse describes primary avenues of karmic support, relationships and activities through which one can work out karmic situations, the house of the initial eclipse is associated with subsidiary matters that supplement prenatal eclipse affairs. With his prenatal eclipse in the eleventh house, Paul can look upon his friends and the groups to which he belongs as primary resources which he can utilize in dealing with karmic obligations. The fifth house, home of the initial eclipse, and its affairs represent secondary avenues of support. Here, universal love as represented by the eleventh house becomes more important to his spiritual growth than romantic love; though both play a role, the lesson of unselfish love is apparent.

Aspects formed by the initial eclipse in the horoscope are

interpreted according to the basic significance of the aspect and the planet or angle, signs and houses involved. These aspects do have a karmic connotation, but their orientation differs from those formed by the prenatal eclipse. They refer mainly to inborn attitudes which may or may not be helpful in building character and nourishing spiritual growth. Easy aspects describe positive attributes developed during prior lifetimes; hard aspects serve as advisories. For instance, a trine between an initial eclipse in Capricorn and a planet in the second house, the ruler of the cusp or Venus, natural ruler of the second house, indicates spiritually correct attitudes toward money and possessions, a positive sense of stewardship that lends to spiritual development along the path shown by the prenatal eclipse. A square involving the same points suggests that avaricious tendencies associated with Capricorn stand in the way of spiritual development and warns against exploitation or misuse of second house assets. The same aspects involving the prenatal eclipse instead of the initial eclipse point to the second house as a direct channel through which one can achieve greater spiritual progress (trine) or as a severe handicap to spiritual growth (square) which calls for concentrated attention in order to overcome second house spiritual barriers.

If, however, the prenatal eclipse forms an aspect with the initial eclipse, initial eclipse aspects assume interpretational emphasis as prenatal eclipse aspects. Regardless of whether or not the two are in aspect, a progressed or transiting aspect to the initial eclipse activates dormant potentials of the prenatal eclipse just as an aspect to the prenatal eclipse does.

Role of The Accompanying Lunar Eclipse

The lunar eclipse which appears in sequence with the prenatal eclipse describes how one instinctively reacts to karmic situations associated with the prenatal eclipse. It deals with inner characteristics inherited from the past which may be so deeply buried in the subconscious that they are not shown by other factors in the natal horoscope. Its type reveals how deeply ingrained these instinctive habits are, with an appulse being the weakest and a partial only slightly stronger. A total lunar eclipse is the strongest which, in the case of positive characteristics, enables the individual to automatically utilize the inner resources with which he or she was born; however, if negative reactions are indicated, it is more difficult for the individual to recognize these qualities and to develop constructive responses.

The sign of the lunar eclipse relates to the manner in which one responds to karmic events and relationships according to the nature of sign qualities as interpreted on a responsive and instinctive level.

The house the lunar eclipse occupies points to affairs and relationships through which one gains spiritual support. This house and its activities also serve as constructive outlets for inner energies.

Easy lunar eclipse aspects within the natal horoscope denote correct instinctual responses, and these are the sort of reactions one tries to utilize and develop more fully. Hard aspects indicate negative instincts that need to be mastered; the stronger the aspect, the harder one must work to correct this innate hindrance to spiritual growth.

The relative position between the lunar eclipse and the prenatal eclipse by sign and in the horoscope bears upon interpretation. Astronomically, only two sign and two house configurations are possible. The sign of the lunar eclipse will lie opposite in the zodiac to that of the prenatal eclipse, or the two eclipses will be placed five signs apart. When they oppose each other by sign, one's manner of expression on the inner plane as described by the lunar eclipse complements sign qual-

16

ities associated with the prenatal eclipse. In effect, sign polarity creates a balance such that one sign provides qualities the other sign lacks. The individual is at a slight disadvantage when the two eclipses are placed five signs apart, as this indicates, no matter how well the lunar eclipse may be aspected, that some adjustment on the inner plane is necessary in order to fully utilize lunar energies in the correct development of karmic affairs as directed by the prenatal eclipse.

Similarly, with the two eclipses occupying opposite houses in the horoscope (not necessarily opposite signs), a supportive situation exists whereby the affairs of the lunar house strengthen activities designated to the house of the prenatal eclipse. When the two eclipses are placed five houses apart, forming an angle of distress, an incongruency between karmic situations depicted by the prenatal eclipse and one's instinctive response to those situations exists.

Various combinations of sign and house alignment are possible, and each are to be interpreted accordingly. The most desirable placement is with signs of both eclipses in polarity and both falling in opposite houses, the configuration shown in Paul's chart (Figure 1). Here we have supportive combinations that balance both manner of expression (signs) and affairs of the houses involved. Generally, though, one must work with eclipses that are inconjunct by sign (five signs apart) yet occupy opposite houses such as appear in Martin's chart (Figure 3), or with eclipses that are in sign polarity but form an angle of distress in the horoscope. In such instances, one must be careful not to confuse manner of expression (signs) with affairs and activities (houses).

A lunar eclipse that precedes the prenatal eclipse has a different emphasis than one that follows. The phase of the Moon during the time interval between the appearance of a preceding lunar eclipse and the following prenatal eclipse covers the waning phase of the Moon, from Full to New Moon, a period of decline that suggests a passive response to prenatal eclipse indications. The lunar eclipse that accompanied Paul's prenatal eclipse (Figure 1) occurred prior to the appearance of his prenatal eclipse. The one that accompanied Martin's prenatal eclipse (Figure 3) followed. The time interval between a prenatal eclipse and an accompanying lunar eclipse that follows covers the waxing phase of the Moon, from prenatal eclipse (New Moon) to Full Moon, a period that can be described as motivating and which suggests initiatory instincts that prompt reactions consistent with overall lunar factors in the chart.

In those rare instances when a prenatal eclipse is accompanied by two lunar eclipses, one appearing two weeks before and the other two weeks following the occurrence of the prenatal eclipse, neither can be ignored or considered more influential per se. Both lunar eclipses must be interpreted in terms of their influence in the chart and their astrological relationship to the prenatal eclipse.

Interpreting the Key Planet

Although the prenatal eclipse reveals clues to any or all prior incarnations and intervals between, the key planet deals only with the immediate prior past life, to the manner of that transition and something about what was carried over from that past life to the present incarnation.

In general, easy aspects formed by the key planet in the natal horoscope point to lessons learned in the immediate past life and karmic assets acquired during that incarnation. Hard aspects depict karmic problems one failed to effectively deal with which need more attention during the current lifetime. The inconjunct, considered a minor aspect by many authorities in natal astrology, is viewed as a major aspect in karmic astrology, one that indicates repetition of the same type of karmic blunders and calls for sincere efforts by the individual to rectify the situation. Meanings of key planet aspects correlate to general aspect interpretation except they are looked upon as connecting links between the immediate past life and the present.

The distance the key planet lies ahead of the prenatal eclipse in the zodiac defines the time period between the last transition and the present rebirth. The number of degrees of arc separating the two points equates to one year of time; one minute equals approximately six days plus two hours. By working backwards from the present birth date and interpolating for minutes of arc, one can arrive at the approximate date of the last transition. It has been generally accepted that the average number of years between one birth and the next rebirth is 144 years, with 72 years allotted to the earth plane and 72 years to the higher plane. However, studies indicate that many people spend much longer than the average on one plane or the other, and some people reincarnate very quickly, in a matter of days or even hours. An almost immediate reincarnation is associated with sudden death due to accident or an act of violence that occurs to an individual unprepared for transition. According to Figure 1, Chapter 1, Paul apparently reincarnated in about 15 years, 7 months and 3 days give or take a day or so (15 degrees and 35 minutes separating his key planet and prenatal eclipse) after his last transition, whereas Martin spent a much longer time on the higher plane, almost 112 years (See Figure 3).

The key planet, by its nature as it operates in the sign and house it occupies, yields information as to the cause of death at the last transition. Its aspects give more details, with an afflicted malefic connected with the natal eighth house associated with an accident (Mars) criminal act (Pluto), suicide (Neptune), or other unnatural cause as described by the aspect and planet involved. Uranus always describes some sort of sudden death, violent or not, which can be discerned from related aspects. Easy aspects to planets linked in some way to the eighth house are associated with a natural, peaceful death, indicating that the person was prepared for transition; hard aspects indicate otherwise.

Although Paul's natal Sun (key planet) closely squares Mars (natural co-ruler of the eighth house), it forms a tighter sextile with natal Jupiter, ruler of the natal eighth house cusp in his chart, suggesting that transition was from natural causes, perhaps from liver trouble or another Jupiterian related ailment. The closest aspect Martin's key planet (Venus) forms is with Pluto, natural ruler of the eighth house posited in the fourth natal house, a trine within 17 minutes of partile, suggests not only that he was prepared for transition (Pluto also rules the afterlife) but that he probably died at home. Venus' wider natal square with Saturn, ruler of the natal eighth house, would suggest that he suffered from a chronic ailment and, in view of the Pluto trine, death was welcomed as a release.

One's sex in the immediate past life corresponds to the gender of the key planet with one exception. Mercury. Because Mercury is androgynous, it takes on the sex of the sign it occupies. The feminine planets are the Moon, Venus and Neptune; masculine planets are the Sun, Mars, Jupiter, Saturn, Uranus and Pluto. Some astrologers view Pluto as feminine. Considering the fact that more males are born, even though more females survive, it is logical to surmise that planetary gender is weighted toward the masculine side.

Note that Paul, with the Sun as his key planet, was a male in his immediate past life; Martin, with Venus as his key planet, was a female.

The key planet is also descriptive of the previous personality and the station one held during that lifetime. Several possibilities exist as each planet has diverse attributes. For instance, the Moon as key planet not only denotes a female personality, but might also describe one who had strong Cancerian qualities and probably was a member of the common populace. The Sun is associated with a male of aristocratic lineage; Mercury suggests the intellectual or writer; Venus, a princess or member of a harem; Mars, an adventurer or military man; Jupiter, a member of the clergy; Saturn, a politician; Uranus, a scientist or radical rabble rouser; Neptune, a seafarer; Pluto, a powerful figure whose aspects give clues as to whether this power was used for good or ill.

These are just a few of numerous possibilities. Keep in mind that each planet is associated with multiple characteristics and, in analyzing its meaning as it refers to a past life, all ramifications must be considered within the framework of the house and sign the planet occupies and its aspects.

Chapter 3

Prenatal Eclipse
in the Signs

The sign occupied by a prenatal eclipse influences hundreds of thousands of people who share that prenatal eclipse. Sign expression is reflected in common interests, the causes these people espouse and the movements they support. Widely separated by distance, few of these people back the same causes, but many participate in movements that share similar objectives. For example, many who share a Taurus prenatal eclipse tend to get involved in groups interested in the arts or finances. A shared prenatal eclipse in Sagittarius may suggest interest in organized religious movements and/or higher education. Common prenatal eclipse interests that do not manifest in the current life cycle remain dormant motivations that stem from a past life and which surface in a future incarnation.

Despite similarities in sign expression among the many, sign qualities are not expressed in the exact same way in any two natal horoscopes. If the prenatal eclipse sign contains a dominant planet(s) or angle, or is heavily populated, its attributes will emerge more strongly than if it is devoid of planets or intercepted. Too, if other factors in the horoscope display similar characteristics, they will reinforce like qualities in sign expression. Positive sign attributes manifest naturally when the prenatal eclipse is well aspected. Afflictions bring out negative sign traits, and it is part of the individual's karmic responsibility to curb such tendencies and to try to develop positive sign characteristics. The dispositor of the prenatal eclipse (the planet that rules the sign it occupies) influences the prenatal eclipse and has bearing upon sign expression as do sign decan and duad sub-rulers and the initial eclipse.

Sign triplicity cannot be overlooked, as it lends a particular focus to prenatal eclipse expression. The triplicity to which the sign occupied by the prenatal eclipse belongs reveals those aspects of the personality that one has failed to develop to full potential or has misused in past lives and which need attention during the current life cycle. This does not mean that other potentials be neglected; it does suggest, however, that it is essential to karmic progress that certain characteristics be fully developed and utilized in the present incarnation.

The triplicity also points out the most suitable manner by which to address karmic problems in order to resolve them. If the natal horoscope reveals attributes similar to those identified by the prenatal eclipse triplicity, the individual naturally responds to its direction. If, however, natal traits and triplicity indications conflict, the individual must work harder to fulfill the obligation to develop these characteristics along positive lines and utilize them constructively. When read in context of the natal horoscope and compared with other prenatal eclipse findings, triplicity implications assume a more personal connotation.

Triplicities

Prenatal Eclipse in a Fire Sign

A prenatal eclipse in a fire sign calls for development and utilization of the creative, inspirational, enterprising aspects of the personality. One must not allow natural creative talent to lie fallow. To do so stunts personal growth and hinders karmic evolution. This position indicates the need for a positive, decisive, self-directed approach to karmic problems. It is most difficult for persons who tend to flow with the tide or sweep problems under the rug and the creatures of habit who resist change to overcome karmic failings and reach the full potential of the current life cycle. With this placement, once one acquires the incentive and courage to take the first steps toward resolving karmic problems, things begin to fall into place. With each karmic step, it becomes easier for the individual to exercise self-initiative and follow through with positive action.

Prenatal Eclipse in an Earth Sign

In an earth sign, a prenatal eclipse emphasizes physical aspects of the personality and one's material values and desires. It directs one to take proper care of the body, to develop and use natural physical abilities and to correctly utilize material resources. It warns against abuse of the body, neglect of health care, laziness, avarice and squandering of material assets. With this placement, persistence, self- reliance and constructive effort form the basis for approaching and resolving karmic problems. There is no quick solution or easy way out, no short cuts. In some instances, the greater part of a lifetime is spent in erasing serious karmic debts. Learning experiences teach self-discipline and responsible application of one's physical talents and material resources, lessons of stewardship one has apparently failed to master in past lives.

Prenatal Eclipse in an Air Sign

A prenatal eclipse in an air sign stresses the need to fully develop and utilize mental abilities and communication skills. It places logic above personal attitudes and emotional leanings in the decision-making process and mandates the exercise of rational thought and fluent expression of ideas. This placement demands that one employ sound judgment based upon fact and truth, that one refuse to be swayed by popular opinions or personal biases. If the horoscope shows motivations to be strongly emotional in nature, it is difficult for that person to develop the objectivity that this prenatal eclipse requires. It is essential, with a prenatal eclipse in an air sign, that one approach karmic problems from an intellectual, unprejudiced, dispassionate point of view if they are to be resolved and not compounded.

Prenatal Eclipse in a Water Sign

When occupying a water sign, a prenatal eclipse points to the need to develop the inner nature. One must learn to experience and express positive emotions, to reach out to others with feeling and empathy, and to channel psychic powers into spiritually correct avenues. This placement carries strong spiritual significance, and strongly indicates that one can overcome spiritual hurdles that have stalled them on the path to enlightenment. It heralds a life cycle devoted primarily to spiritual growth. Karmic progress depends upon evolvement of unselfish attitudes as well as the capacity to place affairs of the world in proper perspective, a difficult task for one whose drives as depicted in the horoscope center around needs for worldly status and creature comforts. The key to resolving karmic problems rests with a selfless approach and consideration of the spiritual aspects of such situations.

Sign Influence

The meanings of the signs given here are based upon pure sign expression as it relates to the prenatal eclipse. Interpretation is colored by the influence of the decan and duad sub-rulers as well as its dispositor and the initial eclipse, and those modifications are to be considered by the reader. Although relationship possibilities are mentioned in connection with pre-natal eclipse signs, signs do not point to specific relationships. Rather, they act as supplementary factors which confirm major indications found elsewhere in the chart.

Prenatal Eclipse in Aries

Activity associated with a prenatal eclipse in Aries reflects the ardor, enthusiasm, courage and daring symbolic of the sign and its planetary ruler, Mars. Expression is spirited and com-petitive. This placement directs one to openly and boldly con-front circumstances represented by the prenatal eclipse and urges one to exercise initiative and leadership in these affairs. Unless other factors in the horoscope contradict, people with an Aries prenatal eclipse are seldom intimidated by any diffi-culties it describes. Rather, they usually view such problems as challenges and approach them accordingly. The approach of the highly competitive individual is sometimes too aggressive, that of the self-willed—too headstrong, and that of the quick—tempered—too angry. In any such instances, resultant action is apt to create problems greater than those which ex-isted initially. This sign position warns against arrogance, bel-ligerence, foolhardiness and other negative Arian traits.

In a woman's chart, an Aries prenatal eclipse may describe a karmic relationship with a husband or lover. In a man's chart, male relatives may play a karmic role. In any case, a karmic re-lationship cannot be definitely established without further and more specific information.

Many people who share an Aries prenatal eclipse also share interest in militant causes and/or organizations devoted to body building and physical fitness.

Prenatal Eclipse in Taurus

Endurance, patience and reliability are among positive at-tributes emphasized by a prenatal eclipse in Taurus. It advocates a firm, persistent stand against obstacles signified by its afflictions and advises determined, continuous effort directed into the affairs it influences. It is important that the individual's attitude toward prenatal eclipse affairs not be so rigid, so resistant to change that he or she fails to adjust to various karmic situations. The accent here is on perseverance, not intractability. The same approach or the same method of treatment win not resolve different types of problems. Even though the necessary effort is applied to prenatal eclipse affairs, endeavors that do not meet the specific requirements of a particular situation result in a karmic standstill and possibly a karmic setback. In order for a person whose prenatal eclipse occupies Taurus to achieve karmic progress, constant effort and karmic need must correspond. Too, if bullheaded-ness, inflexibility, indolence, extravagance or other negative qualities associated with Taurus and its planetary ruler, Venus, manifest, they must be redirected along productive lines.

In a man's chart, a Taurus prenatal eclipse suggests a karmic relationship involving a wife or lover; in a woman's horoscope, it points to female relatives.

Artistic movements and economic causes attract many people who share this prenatal eclipse.

Prenatal Eclipse in Gemini

A prenatal eclipse in Gemini is associated with mental versatility, logic and fluency to the degree described by natal potentials when positive qualities of the sign and its planetary ruler, Mercury, emerge.

The naturally taciturn individual will communicate ideas in fewer words than the more talkative person, and this is to be expected. The main emphasis rests with the capacity to think out a problem situation logically and to express thoughts coherently, not in the style of communicating. It is difficult for those people who are primarily physically or emotionally motivated to respond fully to this prenatal eclipse. The negative mode of Gemini expression produces loquacity, superficiality and caprice. The tendency to embark upon a talkathon without giving the situation the forethought necessary to arrive at a logical solution may manifest. Less desirable Gemini traits tend to splinter or otherwise render ineffectual prenatal eclipse activity, thus hindering karmic progress. The natural Gemini reasoning ability is an asset to be applied to karmic issues.

This sign position can corroborate a sibling relationship defined by other karmic elements shown in the chart.

Groups that promote intellectual awareness or those that conduct polls, distribute questionnaires or gather information by other means attract many who share a Gemini prenatal eclipse.

Prenatal Eclipse in Cancer

With a prenatal eclipse in Cancer, a fluid and sensitive sign, one's reaction to prenatal eclipse directives depends in part upon other signs and planets with which the prenatal eclipse is configurated, for this sign and its planetary ruler, the Moon, respond strongly to and assume coloring of astrological factors that influence them. In any case, Cancerian expression exhibits feeling, receptivity and imagination. This position advises that one become attuned emotionally and spiritually to relationships and situations associated with the prenatal eclipse and to conflicts described by its afflictions in order to gain inner perspectives essential to karmic progress. A prenatal eclipse in Cancer having psychic significance in itself, also reinforces other psychic potentials shown in the natal horoscope. Emotional extremes associated with negative Cancerian expression represent stumbling blocks to karmic development. The inclination to withdraw emotionally from prenatal eclipse affairs, to bide in the shell of the crab so to speak, precludes growth. At the other end of the emotional spectrum, the tendency to become overly attached emotionally, to become too emotionally involved in prenatal eclipse interests has a similar retarding effect.

This placement is suggestive of karmic family ties and, perhaps, maternal karmic links.

Numbers of people who share a prenatal eclipse in Cancer gravitate into movements that support family life or display interest in genealogical societies.

Prenatal Eclipse in Leo

A prenatal eclipse in Leo indicates the need to exercise leadership and authority in the karmic situations it describes. Vigor and resolve are essential to the correct treatment of problems associated with prenatal eclipse afflictions. A half-hearted approach gains nothing. Creativity, self-confidence and vitality are among assets one can utilize if positive Leo qualities develop, qualities associated with its planetary ruler, the Sun. It is difficult for the naturally diffident person who lacks self-assurance to master prenatal eclipse affairs and achieve karmic progress; it is just as difficult for the self-centered, for egocentricity thwarts karmic growth. With this placement, it is important that one recognize the difference between self-confidence, a plus, and self-centeredness, a minus. Vainglory, ostentation, pomposity and other negative Leo characteristics represent stumbling blocks to karmic growth. It is necessary to growth that one keep less desirable Leo traits in check and utilize positive Leo attributes. Failure to do either retards development of prenatal eclipse affairs.

This sign position may confirm a paternal karmic relationship or one with offspring.

Youth groups such as Scouts or the Teen League and causes

that promote the welfare of children (child development programs, anti-child abuse movements, etc.) appeal to many who share a Leo prenatal eclipse.

Prenatal Eclipse in Virgo

In Virgo, prenatal eclipse activity exhibits the work ethic, circumspection and discrimination. When positive attributes of the sign and its planetary ruler, Mercury, emerge, dedication, discernment and a strong sense of duty underscore one's efforts in affairs influenced by the prenatal eclipse. In addition to the physical demands associated with all prenatal eclipses that appear in earth signs, this placement also calls for an analytical approach to problems defined by prenatal eclipse afflictions and to other karmic situations it describes. It is important that one be observant and perceptive in these affairs, yet not place too much emphasis on insignificant details. The tendency to continually criticize along with other excessive perfectionist traits manifest as negative Virgo qualities which hinder Karmic progress. The caution this sign position provokes is regarded as a karmic asset unless carried to extremes. Inordinate restraint results in the failure to act in prenatal eclipse affairs and thus stalls karmic growth. Health problems that manifest in the current lifetime may be rooted in a past life, so this possibility should be studied from all angles when one's prenatal eclipse is in Virgo.

This sign placement suggests the possibility of a karmic tie with an aunt or uncle.

Numbers of people who share a Virgo prenatal eclipse support movements devoted to better health and/or improved working conditions.

Prenatal Eclipse in Libra

With a prenatal eclipse in Libra, intellectual motivation common to air signs is softened by harmonious and artistic qualities indigenous to this sign and its planetary ruler, Venus. Positive prenatal eclipse expression is pleasing, impartial and intelligent. With this placement, fair play and cooperation are important to the successful resolution of problems described by prenatal eclipse afflictions and in the handling of other prenatal eclipse affairs. Relationships play a large role in development. The individual with a prenatal eclipse in Libra usually attracts as partners and other close associates people with whom he or she shares karmic ties, and these people are instrumental in shared karmic achievements and failures. The individual who allows the partner to exert more than a fair share of influence in a relationship or who resorts to extensive appeasement in order to preserve the relationship does so at the risk of compromising karmic progress. Insincerity, spinelessness and self-indulgence are among negative Libra traits which, if allowed to develop, interfere with karmic growth.

This placement highly suggests that a marriage or other close association is karmic in nature. It may also point to the possibility of a karmic tie with a niece or nephew.

Groups whose interests center around art appreciation and causes that promote world justice attract many people whose prenatal eclipse is in Libra.

Prenatal Eclipse in Scorpio

The intensity and passion symbolic of Scorpio and its planetary ruler, Pluto (the higher octave of Mars), predominate expression of a prenatal eclipse that occupies that sign. Strength of purpose undergirds prenatal eclipse expression. Scorpio's gift of probing insight enables one to discern root causes of karmic situations and problems. It is up to the individual to use this innate knowledge to gain karmic progress or not. Enormous karmic gains are possible under the direction of a Scorpio prenatal eclipse if positive elements of the sign are utilized and negative qualities subdued. Without control, baser Scorpio sexual urges can erupt, vengeance and cruelty manifest, hatred develop. The desire for retribution against wrongs may override the capacity for forgiveness. A negative response to this prenatal eclipse can compound karmic debts that take several incarnations to erase, effectively obliterating karmic strides achieved in past lifetimes. A positive response leads to a high level of spiritual evolution which prepares one for the ultimate stages of spiritual growth. Thus it is extremely important that the individual whose prenatal eclipse is posited in Scorpio study its significance and respond along positive lines according to its direction.

Those people to whom one is drawn sexually may share karmic ties with a person whose prenatal eclipse is in Scorpio.

Group interests for these people include the afterlife, reincarnation and human sexuality.

Prenatal Eclipse in Sagittarius

Activity of a prenatal eclipse that occupies Sagittarius is expressed with the enthusiasm, frankness and profusion common to the sign and its planetary ruler, Jupiter. The free-ranging style of Sagittarius provides for a broad spectrum of interest; however, it is important with this placement that one focalize attention as specified by prenatal eclipse indications and not scatter efforts frivolously if karmic progress is to be achieved. A Sagittarius prenatal eclipse is associated with the search for ultimate truths, the development of spiritual philosophy and the gaining of spiritual wisdom. Motivation for action in affairs influenced by this prenatal eclipse stems from moral concepts and/or religious convictions that are holdovers from a past life and which may or may not be spiritually correct. Therefore, it is essential that one examine such motivations and correct those that are out of harmony with karmic requirements so that growth can be achieved. Karmic endeavors based upon misplaced idealism or misguided beliefs are ineffective. When negative sign traits emerge, some people magnify karmic problems. Exaggerated efforts that follow overshoot the mark. Others, because of false optimism, underestimate karmic situations and their efforts fall short.

This placement suggests a karmic relationship with a grandchild or perhaps an in-law.

Many people with a Sagittarius prenatal eclipse are drawn toward organized religions, mental expansion groups or the study of foreign cultures.

Prenatal Eclipse in Capricorn

A prenatal eclipse in Capricorn advises a serious approach to related affairs and stresses conservative, conscientious expression. In order to achieve karmic progress, one must overcome self-indulgent tendencies and master the self-discipline symbolic of this sign and its planetary ruler, Saturn. This placement identifies the old soul whose mission is to teach others that they may grow in enlightenment. Because of the constrictive, avaricious, selfish qualities associated with Capricorn, some people whose prenatal eclipse occupies this sign find it difficult to reach out as teachers or to lead the kind of life that others admire from a spiritual standpoint. However, failure to do so impedes karmic development. The concerned individual strives to correct wrongful karmic situations and to guide others along the spiritual path. This placement can be regarded as an opportunity to gain substantial karmic advances, but the price is dedication and hard work, often at the expense of personal pleasure and worldly prestige.

Capricornian relationships are linked to authority figures which may be the father or another person whom the individual looks up to.

Most people who share a prenatal eclipse in Capricorn join business or professional organizations and many show interest in government affairs.

Prenatal Eclipse in Aquarius

The unprejudiced attitudes and human concern associated with Aquarius and its planetary ruler, Uranus (higher octave of Mercury), provide a foundation for spiritual growth and karmic understanding when a prenatal eclipse occupies this sign. Aquarian expression reflects an open-minded, timely approach to karmic situations. The past is not viewed as a burden that one has created and now must bear, but it is looked upon as a key to present karmic needs and a guide to future development. A person with this prenatal eclipse in the horoscope has a unique opportunity to change the karmic course he or she has embarked upon if that person so desires. A prenatal eclipse in Aquarius does warn against precipitous actions, those steps one sometimes takes to satisfy the need to be different without a specific goal in mind. This sign placement encourages an innovative approach and novel solutions to karmic problems, but such actions must be geared to fit the situation to which they are directed. Whimsical changes and contradictory efforts interrupt karmic progress and add to the accumulation of karmic debts.

Relationships that imply karmic links include sons-in-law and daughters-in-law as well as friends.

People who share a prenatal eclipse in Aquarius usually find humanitarian groups and futuristic organizations appealing. Most show much interest in astrology and related sciences.

Prenatal Eclipse in Pisces

A prenatal eclipse in Pisces indicates that one is nearing the highest step in the particular spiritual level he or she has achieved. The current lifetime marks a period in which to complete that level in preparation for embarking on the next highest phase of karmic development. It is important here that one is neither blinded by the illusionary qualities of the sign and its planetary ruler, Neptune (higher octave of Venus), nor lured into spiritual escapism. If negative Piscean attributes manifest, one may flounder through karmic situations without ever realizing that his or her action is futile. Some may never recognize the karmic implications of associated problems and relationships. Spiritual awareness that fosters well-directed efforts is essential to karmic growth. This placement warns against the use of so-called mind-enhancing drugs as a means of achieving spiritual communion. Meditation can be helpful in gaining spiritual enlightenment.

Because of the very secrecy associated with Pisces, it is difficult to discern Piscean relationships; but a prenatal eclipse in Pisces may clarify a possible karmic relationship shown elsewhere in the chart.

Most who share a prenatal eclipse in Pisces also share interest in the esoteric, especially those branches dealing with spiritualism and dream interpretation.

Intercepted Signs

When the prenatal eclipse falls in an intercepted sign in the natal horoscope, the implication is that something of a karmic nature is hidden. It may be very difficult for one to uncover these veiled factors, but the responsibility rests with the individual to bring them out and work with whatever the prenatal eclipse is indicating. Failure to recognize and resolve karmic issues can create a karmic stalemate. As the chart progresses and the interception disappears, one finds it easier to break the pattern of karmic status quo and tackle the problems at hand. However, developmental opportunities missed because of lack of awareness are not apt to recur, so it behooves the individual to thoroughly analyze the intercepted prenatal eclipse to discover its hidden message and follow its directives.

Chapter 4

Prenatal Eclipse
in the Houses

The natal house the prenatal eclipse calls home is the most important karmic house in the horoscope, even though its affairs may not in the usual sense be duly significant to spiritual evolution. The presence of the prenatal eclipse in a house elevates that house to one of spiritual significance, and the activities and relationships it represents offer the basis for karmic growth. This house provides resources upon which the individual can draw to supplement his or her own endeavors to gain progress on the karmic wheel.

Each house, in combination with its cusp ruler, its natural ruler and the planets contained therein, is representative of numerous avenues open to the individual in pursuit of spiritual growth. Before studying the finer details of each house and associated factors, one considers the general mode and function of the house as it applies to karmic astrology.

Functional Houses

Functional houses are grouped into four sets of three houses, each of which displays a different aspect of the same common function. Think of a tree with three branches, each representing one element of the primary function which composes the whole (tree). For example. Individual Houses (one, five and nine) represent the Tree of Life with the first house representing the physical body, the fifth the soul, and the ninth the spirit. This is the Tree of Life.

Temporal houses (two, six and ten) are associated with worldly interests and are referred to karmically as the Tree of Substance. In this framework, the second house is associated with wealth, the sixth with work, and the tenth with career.

Relative houses (three, seven and eleven) collectively called the Tree of Associations, point to relationships. In this sense, the third represents relatives, the seventh partners, and the eleventh friends.

Esoteric houses (fourth, eighth and twelfth) depict the Tree of Evolution. Here, the fourth is associated with the subconscious, the eighth with the afterlife, and the twelfth with karma (Figure 5), Keep these general functions in mind when applying the basic meanings of your prenatal eclipse in the house it occupies in your horoscope.

Modal Houses

Another general house classification to be considered is that of the modal houses. These houses are grouped in three sets of four houses each. These sets have an orientation different from functional sets. Rather than a common function, modal sets share a common mode of activity. Angular houses (one, four, seven and ten) are classed as the more initiatory and dynamic of the houses within the framework of the horoscope, the houses which provide the strongest motivation for action.

Succedent houses (two, five, eight and eleven) represent the workers of the zodiac who carry on and complete that which is initiated in the angular houses. These houses are considered productive houses.

Individual Houses 1, 5, 9

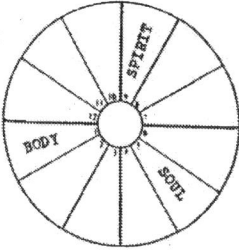

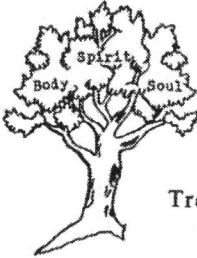

SPIRIT
BODY
SOUL

Tree of Life

Spirit
Body Soul

Temporal Houses 2, 6, 10

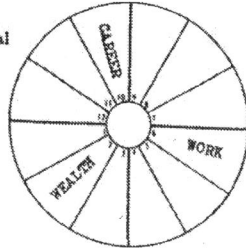

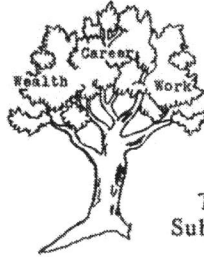

CAREER
WORK
WEALTH

Tree of Substance

Career
Wealth Work

Relative Houses 3, 7, 11

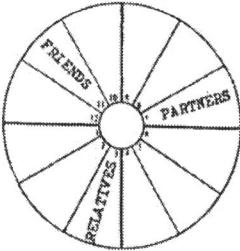

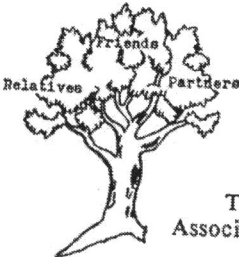

FRIENDS
PARTNERS
RELATIVES

Tree of Associations

Friends
Relatives Partners

Esoteric Houses 4, 8, 12

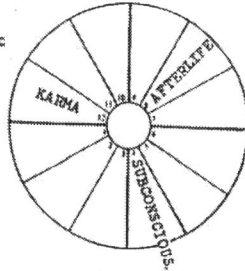

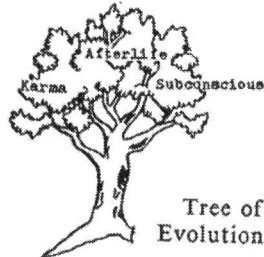

KARMA
AFTERLIFE
SUBCONSCIOUS

Tree of Evolution

Afterlife
Karma Subconscious

Figure 5   Functional Houses

41

Cadent hoses (three, six, nine and twelve) are known as dispersive houses which disseminate that which has been initiated in angular houses and produced in succedent houses. These are the houses of transmittal.

House Resources

The resources of the house occupied by the prenatal eclipse are at the disposal of the individual. The avenues of support so described may be modified or supplemented according to the sign on the cusp and its planetary ruler, the natural planetary ruler of the house, planets posited in that house and aspects involving that house. House classifications, functional and modal, also color interpretation.

Prenatal Eclipse in the Natal First House

The person whose prenatal eclipse falls in the first house is placed in a position of self-responsibility. An individual and angular house, the first represents the person and self-motivation. People with this placement must seek self-awareness and self-identity. They must learn to recognize and understand themselves as individuals and accept themselves for what they are before they can grow spiritually. Acknowledging one's character defects and recognizing one's positive attributes are essential to further development. Those who blind themselves to spiritually incorrect attitudes and fail to properly utilize personal potentials create a self-imposed karmic stalemate.

The first step, that of recognizing innate faults as well as positive characteristics, is the most difficult. Once one realizes who and what they are, they can begin the process of fulfilling karmic responsibilities. Unlike the other houses, one's greatest karmic resource and support is himself or herself. This placement compares to a karmic do-it-yourself kit. Once you begin the process, others will jump on the bandwagon to help you out.

The keys to spiritual enlightenment and karmic progress are almost totally in the hands of the person whose prenatal eclipse falls in the first house, and it is entirely up to that individual to embark upon the charted course. Aspects to planets associated with other houses provide a backup system if one falters, but it is up to the individual to take the first steps toward erasing karmic debts and utilizing karmic assets.

Prenatal Eclipse in the Natal Second House

A prenatal eclipse in the second house, a temporal and succedent house, emphasizes tangible assets. One's money and possessions, regardless of worldly worth, are looked upon as karmic resources. Apparently, one has acquired spiritually correct material values and an innate sense of stewardship in past lives and has mastered personal greed and avarice. It is important with this placement that one not slip back into a pattern of materialism which places worldly goods above the needs of humanity. There is nothing wrong with attempting to improve one's economic status and build substantial assets. The essential point here lies in the way one goes about obtaining wealth and how one utilizes the material resources at hand. Honesty is a foremost requirement in all financial dealings. One is advised to follow the instincts with which he or she was born when it comes to money matters and not be lured into the worldly trap of obtaining money and possessions at the expense of others. To do so creates a karmic setback; one loses ground, so to speak.

It is most important that one not be selfish with worldly goods, yet it is just as important that one not be gullible as to how and with whom these goods are shared.

The second house also has a sexual connotation as described by its natural sign, Taurus, and its natural ruler, Venus, which exemplify the receptive sexual nature. This placement indicates that one has gained the proper perspective between charitable love and sexual attraction, a karmic asset to be utilized.

Prenatal Eclipse in the Natal Third House

With a prenatal eclipse in the third house, a relative and cadent house, a person's strongest karmic resources are the intellect and communicative potentials with which he or she was born. It is of the utmost importance to karmic progress that these assets be fully developed and utilized. Logic and reasoning powers are karmic tools earned in the past, tools to be used in determining the correct spiritual course to follow and in resolving karmic problems. It is important that the individual endeavor to continue to learn during the present lifetime through study or experience, to broaden mental horizons and to exercise sound judgment in all matters. Moreover, one is called upon to spread the message of karma, to give hope to the hopeless, to inform the ignorant.

One's relatives, especially siblings, provide support and guidance if one is willing to accept their help. The neighborhood, too, is a source of karmic support. If one feels ill at ease, a misfit in the local environment, it is imperative that he or she move to a more comfortable area, one which gives that person a sense of belonging.

This placement indicates a possible karmic relationship with a brother or sister. Aspects to Mercury or a planet in Gemini give further support to the supposition. However, one can only be sure if the relationship is corroborated by prenatal eclipse ties between the individual's horoscope and that of another party as discussed in Chapter 7.

Prenatal Eclipse in the Natal Fourth House

An individual whose prenatal eclipse occupies the fourth house, an esoteric and angular house, has a karmic advantage because this house which is associated with inner instincts and the subconscious gives one an inborn sense of what the prenatal eclipse is all about. There is a natural attraction to the spiritual aspects of life and a subconscious motivation to face karmic responsibilities. One's inner resources are assets that one can rely upon to recognize and correctly deal with karmic situations. The doubting person may choose to ignore inner promptings and thus miss out on opportunities to achieve spiritual strides, but even the most skeptical are drawn toward spiritual affairs though they may deny the fact and refuse to follow through with action. However, those who heed the message of the prenatal eclipse can gain enormous progress on the karmic wheel.

This placement indicates that the parental home provides a setting which fosters spiritual growth. The family in general and the mother in particular represent a support system which promotes one's development.

A prenatal eclipse in the fourth house strongly indicates karmic family ties. An aspect from the Moon or a planet in Cancer to the prenatal eclipse points to the mother, one to the Sun or a planet in Leo to the father, and one to Mercury or a planet in Gemini to a sibling. Additional confirming factors are necessary to verify the relationship.

Prenatal Eclipse in the Natal Fifth House

One does not usually look upon the fifth house as a spiritually oriented house, but by virtue of its planetary ruler, the Sun, it is representative of the soul, that part of the personality that lives on after the body (first house) dies. At transition, the soul finds a home on a higher plane until it is prepared for rebirth on (he earthly plane.

A prenatal eclipse in the fifth house, a relative and succedent house, embodies the eternal life principle and love.

It instructs one to elevate the selfish love associated with that house to the higher form of humanitarian love described by its opposite house, the eleventh. The need to love and be loved is part of human nature. With this placement, it is important that one learn the lesson of unselfish love.

In the natal horoscope, the fifth house is associated primarily with selfish needs. One seeks self satisfaction through love affairs, procreation and worldly pleasures. With the prenatal eclipse here, one must overcome selfish desires and utilize fifth house assets in a manner productive of karmic progress. One's natural creative expression is a karmic resource to be developed along lines consistent with spiritual growth.

Fifth house placement of the prenatal eclipse indicates that one gains spiritual support from offspring, and there may be karmic ties that link the individual with his or her own children.

Prenatal Eclipse in the Natal Sixth House

In the sixth house, a temporal and cadent house, a prenatal eclipse focuses on the work ethic, the need to serve others, work relationships, job conditions and health. Proper care of the body is essential to physical well being as well as to spiritual development. Neglect of physical needs impairs one's ability to serve, and it is through unselfish service to one's fellow man that the individual gains the greatest karmic progress and spiritual growth.

With this placement, it is important that the individual's workplace be compatible with his or her nature. Whether one's workplace is in the home, a factory, an office or other site of employment is not the important factor here. The atmosphere, the environment in which one spends a great deal of time influences that person's capacity to function at full potential both physically and spiritually. Ill health and stunted spiritual growth can be a direct result of working in uncongenial surroundings. Too, hypochondria can manifest, especially if Neptune or a planet in Pisces aspects the prenatal eclipse.

The workplace and job associates should provide a support system helpful to karmic progress. If the individual feels like a misfit in job surroundings, it is spiritually advantageous to change employment.

Sixth house placement of the prenatal eclipse also suggests possible karmic ties with an aunt or uncle.

Prenatal Eclipse in the Natal Seventh House

A prenatal eclipse that occupies the seventh house, a relative and angular house, places emphasis upon related-ness and interaction on a one-to-one basis. Both marital and business partnerships as well as contracts and agreements are within the province of this house. Note that paperwork and the signing of contractual documents are a third house function, but the essence of any pact or compromise comes under the dominion of the seventh house. It is through this house that one seeks a counterpart, a person who completes the lacks in one's own being so that the two become a whole to form an entity comprised of complementary qualities bound together in the union of two special human beings. It is toward the goal of unity that one is directed to strive with a seventh house prenatal eclipse.

Cooperation is essential to karmic growth when the prenatal eclipse occupies the seventh house. It is important that the individual learn to give priority to the needs of others above his or her own personal desires. It is also important that one contribute as much to a seventh house relationship as the partner does. This is not a one-sided situation where one person is the taker and the other the giver; a fair share of give and take is the desirable objective.

Spiritual support stems from the marital relationship and other dose associations. Possible karmic links with one's spouse, business partner or a niece or nephew are also signified.

Prenatal Eclipse in the Natal Eighth House

Posited in the eighth house, an esoteric and succedent house, a prenatal eclipse carries a significant karmic message. This house deals with physical death, the afterlife and rebirth. Therefore, what one does in terms of prenatal eclipse directives is of utmost importance, for the eighth house links the past, present and future. This position can be a precarious one. In a sense it represents a testing ground for karmic gains acquired in the past. Plutonian temptations are available to the individual as well as the resources represented by the higher form of Plutonian and eighth house expression. No doubt, with a prenatal eclipse in the eighth house, one will be tempted by perverse sexual urges, misuse of corporate or jointly owned funds, or lured into criminal activities. A sense of power accompanies an eighth house prenatal eclipse, and it is up to the individual to direct this power into spiritually correct avenues.

When one's prenatal eclipse reaches the eighth house, it indicates that the soul has reached a critical point in spiritual evolution. A higher plane has definitely been attained, but it is up to the individual to sustain spiritual growth and not fall prey to earthly temptations that would cause a backward slide on the karmic wheel.

If the karmic test is failed, one must repeat past learning experiences until correct spiritual attitudes are so deeply ingrained that potential setbacks are thwarted and karmic progress is assured.

Prenatal Eclipse in the Natal Ninth House

An individual and cadent house, the ninth is the home of spirit. Many people and most dictionaries equate spirit with soul. The two terms are not synonymous from a karmic point of view. The soul (fifth house) lives on; the spirit, like the body (first house), ceases to exist at the time of transition. The spirit, as represented by the ninth house, is defined as that intangible higher consciousness through which one develops a spiritual philosophy, built upon motivation stemming from the seventh house and the results of eighth house activities.

A prenatal eclipse that occupies the ninth house not only calls upon the individual to develop spiritually correct attitudes but also to disseminate this knowledge, to spread the word of spiritual evolution. The individual who has not progressed on the karmic wheel may face a predicament. If spiritual development has not reached the point where the individual can be sure of his or her directions, then it is next to impossible to reach out to others in a spiritual sense. Therefore, the first step is to develop the spirit and then proceed to share enlightening thoughts with others.

Grandchildren and in-laws represent a support group on which one can rely upon for assistance in resolving karmic issues. Some of these people may share karmic ties if other factors in the horoscope confirm a karmic relationship.

Prenatal Eclipse in the Natal Tenth House

A prenatal eclipse that occupies the tenth house of the horoscope, a temporal and angular house, implies that one should strive for a reputation of integrity and public service. It is important with this placement that one not put on a facade of honesty and public interest, but that one live up to the demands of public life in a manner consistent with spiritual interests. One's career choice is important with this placement, for the individual will probably be faced with contradictory opportunities—those that foster spiritual growth and those that only promote worldly prospects. In many cases, one can combine both spiritual and worldly pursuits. As long as one maintains a spiritually correct attitude and adheres to proper criteria in professional activities, there is no reason not to strive toward worldly objectives. The error lies in compromising spiritual growth in the interests of worldly success.

The horoscopes of politicians often show a prenatal eclipse in the tenth house. Those that heed the message of the prenatal eclipse introduce policies helpful to their constituents regardless of personal cost in terms of pride or anguish; those that ignore its direction follow a course designed to inflate their prestige, thus incurring severe karmic setbacks.

With this placement, the career setting provides karmic resources upon which one can draw. It also points to karmic ties with the father.

Prenatal Eclipse in the Natal Eleventh House

The eleventh house, a relative and succedent house, represents humanitarian causes and universal love. A prenatal eclipse placed in this house focuses on fellowship and the causes one espouses. A prenatal eclipse in this house offers one the opportunity to grow spiritually through organizations to which they belong, and advises against those groups which are oriented toward selfish or counterproductive purposes. The spirit of brotherhood exemplified by the natural sign of the eleventh house, Aquarius, is important to spiritual development. Although this house represents one's hopes and wishes, those desires of a selfish nature must be put aside and the interests of humanity as a whole placed foremost if spiritual growth is to be attained. The sign of a prenatal eclipse placed in the eleventh house is of special importance because it clarifies expression of one's humanitarian leanings. For example, Paul's prenatal eclipse in Aries (Figure 1) falls in the eleventh house of his natal horoscope. Although the eleventh is a succedent house, the Aries eclipse supplies initiative and motivation.

Social contacts are significant with this placement of the prenatal eclipse. It is through such connections that one gains support in the effort to resolve karmic problems. One's friends and colleagues are considered karmic resources in a very touching way.

A prenatal eclipse in the eleventh house points to possible karmic links with friends and sons-in-law or daughters-in-law.

Prenatal Eclipse in the Natal Twelfth House

The twelfth house, an esoteric and cadent house, is the house of karma. A prenatal eclipse that occupies this house indicates a high level of spiritual development. Because of the very nature of Neptune, planetary ruler of the twelfth house, individuals with a twelfth house prenatal eclipse may blind themselves to karmic realities, especially if negative aspects predominate. Therefore, it is especially important that one realize that he or she is on the verge of completing a karmic phase and closely study the course mapped out by the prenatal eclipse.

Individuals who follow prenatal eclipse directions are assured of karmic progress; those that do not can look forward to, at the very least, another lifetime in which the same problems manifest, perhaps compounded by additional spiritual miscues created in the present life cycle.

It must be noted that deep-seated psychological problems of a karmic nature can manifest with this prenatal eclipse placement. It is the individual's responsibility to recognize and resolve problems of the inner nature. These problems stem from past life errors, and until one can admit the fault, corrective action is futile. Because of the secretive nature of this house, it may be difficult for the individual to discern exactly where the problem lies. The temptation to cover up or deny one's obligations, if it exists, must be overcome. Open confrontation of karmic issues is a must.

Chapter 5

Prenatal Eclipse Aspects in the Natal Horoscope

The aspects formed between the prenatal eclipse and planets and angles point to specific problem areas as well as to karmic assets acquired in the past. Aspects transform the natal horoscope into a karmic map with the prenatal eclipse the starting point and the aspecting planets various destinations one tries to reach in life. It sometimes helps understanding the message of the aspects to draw lines connecting the prenatal eclipse to aspected points in the chart giving a visual picture of the path to spiritual growth (Figures 6 and 7).

It is customary to use natal orbs when aspecting the prenatal eclipse within the natal horoscope. Because opinions on orbs vary, for the purposes of this text the following orbs have been used: conjunction, eight degrees; sextile, six degrees; square, eight degrees; trine, eight degrees; inconjunct, six degrees; opposition, eight degrees. The orb for minor aspects is two degrees, for parallels and contraparallels, one degree.

Major easy aspects describe primary karmic assets, those avenues, attributes and relationships which provide resources with which to work out karmic problems. Easy minor aspects are supplementary in nature.

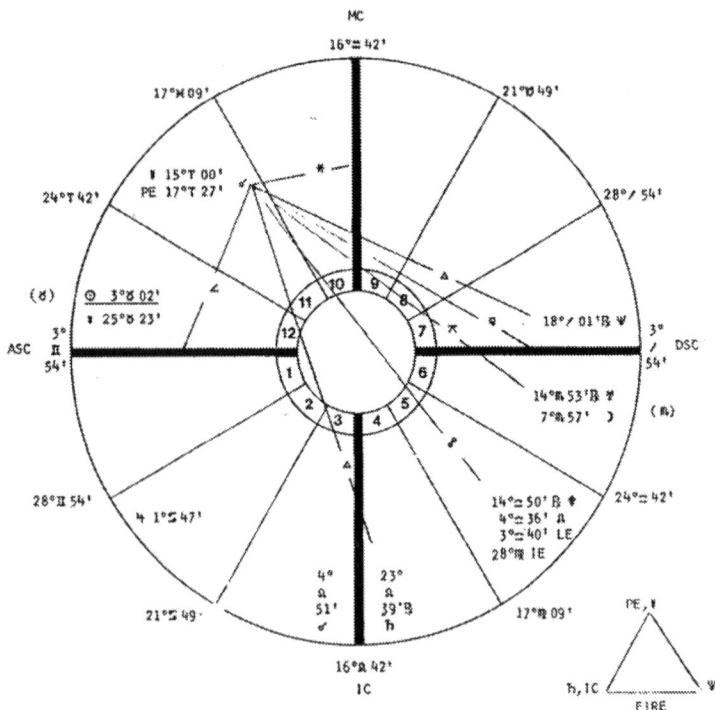

Figure 6   Paul's Karmic Map

Major hard aspects (including the inconjunct) give direct clues to karmic problems and reveal potentials for karmic teaming experiences that can manifest when activated by a progressed or transiting planet. Minor hard aspects refer to minor infractions such as an unkind act that may have caused another person brief pain but does no lasting harm. Wrongful attitudes or habits associated with a minor hard aspect, if not corrected, can build into serious problems.

Parallels and contraparallels act as corroborating factors that verify other karmic factors in the chart.

When interpreting aspects, the signs and houses involved must be considered as well as other aspects to the same points.

54

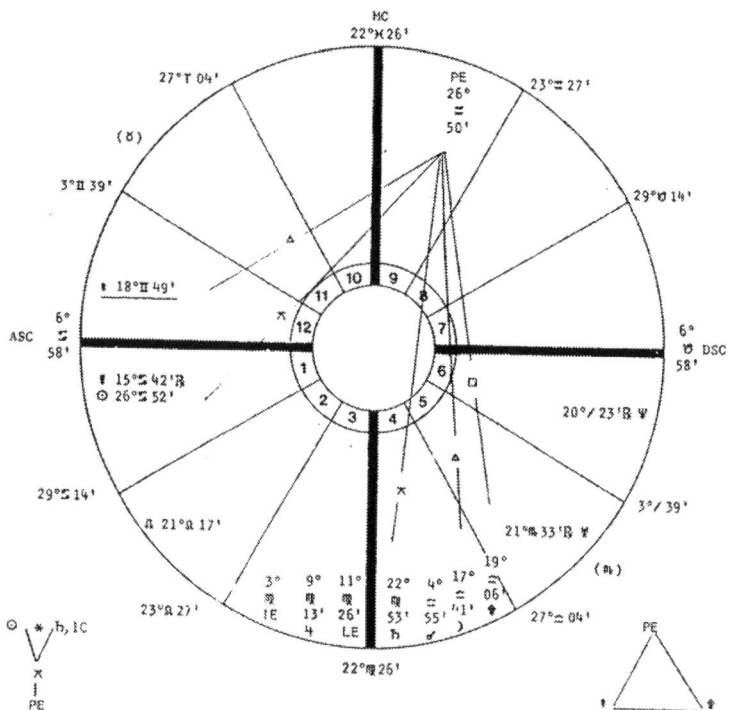

Figure 7   Martin's Karmic Map

Natal Sun Aspects
to the Prenatal Eclipse

Any aspect between the natal Sun and the prenatal eclipse is suggestive of a karmic relationship with the natural father or with offspring, the nature of which corresponds to the nature of the aspect. In a woman's chart, karmic ties with the husband may be indicated.

Natal Sun Conjunct Prenatal Eclipse

This conjunction occurs only in the horoscopes of people born within eight days following the appearance of the prenatal eclipse. It signifies a unification of affairs ruled by the Sun and the house it occupies with activities associated with the prenatal eclipse. If the two are posited in the same house, this house is strengthened as a focal point for prenatal eclipse energies. If the two are placed in adjoining houses, the conjunction unites the affairs of the houses in the manner that marriage joins a man and a woman.

This aspect indicates that the individual has attained self-mastery through past life experiences and is capable of self-motivation within the limits of the sign occupied by the Sun which represents the self, the ego.

Natal Sun Sextile Prenatal Eclipse

A sextile between the Sun and the prenatal eclipse points to positive characteristics as described by the Sun that one has gained through past life experiences. These attributes are to be looked upon as karmic assets and utilized accordingly. The activities and associations governed by the Sun and the house it occupies in the horoscope present opportunities through which one can work out obligations. This house is a house of karmic resource. Linked to the house of the prenatal eclipse by aspect, it is a direct channel available to the individual in resolving karmic issues.

Natal Sun Square Prenatal Eclipse

This aspect denotes self-created obstacles and strictures one has acquired in a past life. It is important here that the individual overcome any egotistical tendencies and learn to put the needs of others before his or her own. The urge to impose one's will upon the will of others must be acknowledged and suppressed. The house occupied by the Sun is a problem area which needs attention. The root cause of karmic situations described therein rests with the individual, and until that person can recognize his or her own responsibility, associated learning experiences may prove of little karmic value.

Natal Sun Trine Prenatal Eclipse

Circumstances conducive to self-development are described by this trine. The individual is advised to further develop the positive qualities associated with the Sun according to its sign placement and to utilize these attributes and the affairs of the house occupied by the Sun in confronting karmic situations. Associated activities and relationships support the personal growth necessary to spiritual growth and ease the path to karmic progress. If this trine forms part of a grand trine, it broadens the scope of karmic resources accordingly.

Natal Sun Inconjunct Prenatal Eclipse

The inconjunct, a karmic aspect in itself, always points to problem situations carried over from several prior lifetimes which have gone unresolved. This aspect tells you that whatever the karmic problem described, it has gone on far too long. Too many opportunities to resolve the problem have been ignored, and the time has come for the individual to face up to the responsibility. Not to do so puts the individual at risk of piling up karmic debts that take several incarnations to erase. Since the Sun is a key factor here, self-improvement and the utilization of leadership qualities are musts in addressing related problems. Note that Martin's natal Sun (Figure 7) forms an inconjunct with his prenatal eclipse which is also inconjunct natal Saturn, completing a yod (natal Sun sextile Saturn) with the prenatal eclipse at the focal point. With his Sun in the first house, responsibility is placed directly upon him to straighten up a karmic situation that probably involves the father and perhaps both parents since the Sun, Saturn and the fourth house (home of Saturn in the chart) are directly connected.

Natal Sun Opposite Prenatal Eclipse

This aspect occurs infrequently, only when one is born dose to the date of the solar eclipse that follows the prenatal eclipse, and even then the forming aspect seldom falls within the allowable orb. The nature of an opposition, a separative aspect, is conflict, and the Sun here indicates that conflict is with the self as well as the affairs of the house occupied by the Sun and those governed by the Sun in the horoscope. This individual has not learned the lessons of self-awareness and self-acceptance. In order to achieve karmic progress, one begins a process that leads to self-recognition, finding one's self-identity and developing a sense of self-worth. Once this has been accomplished, one is equipped to tackle other karmic problems.

Natal Moon Aspects to the Prenatal Eclipse

An aspect between the prenatal eclipse and the natal Moon brings family interests and particularly the maternal relationship into play. The probability of a karmic tie with the mother is evident. In a man's chart, the Moon may refer to his wife.

Natal Moon Conjunct Prenatal Eclipse

The Moon in conjunction with the prenatal eclipse shows an inner understanding of past life experiences and their impact upon the present. This knowledge may be deeply buried within the subconscious; but nevertheless, it manifests in the form of instinct and psychic awareness. This conjunction which unites the Moon and its affairs with the prenatal eclipse is truly a blessing, for if one is not consciously aware of where he or she is at on the karmic wheel and what action to take to insure progress, that person knows instinctively what should be done. The skeptic who chooses to ignore these inklings and continues to repeat mistakes of the past or commit new ones suffers karmic setbacks.

Natal Moon Sextile Prenatal Eclipse

Although the sextile is not as strong as the conjunction, it does create conditions that arouse past life memories which give the individual a sense of karmic direction. It is the house occupied by the Moon and the activities and relationships with which it is associated that assist one's spiritual development. Through its direction, obligations described by the prenatal eclipse can be resolved.

Natal Moon Square Prenatal Eclipse

This square points to emotional blocks that interfere with one's capacity to recognize karmic obligations. Usually, this aspect points to a debt that one does not want to remember because he or she does not want to admit to responsibility. In the past. this person has taken the easy way out, shifted blame on someone else or belittled the seriousness of the offense. The square points to the karmic situation and calls upon the individual to shoulder his or her responsibility and make every effort to resolve the situation. The house occupied by the Moon and other lunar aspects as well as other prenatal eclipse aspects should be studied carefully to determine the exact nature of the karmic barrier.

Natal Moon Trine Prenatal Eclipse

The natural ease of accomplishment associated with the trine enables the individual whose horoscope contains this aspect to reach the inner self, to more readily recognize karmic debts associated with hard prenatal eclipse aspects. Too, this aspect describes circumstances that encourage one to confront karmic issues and makes readily accessible the avenues of resource described by the lunar house, its interests, activities and associations. Conditions are such that one gains the inner strength necessary to promote positive karmic achievement and spiritual growth.

Natal Moon Inconjunct Prenatal Eclipse

This aspect strongly indicates that many times along the path one has met the same type of karmic situation and failed to respond to it effectively. The time to face the issue is now, and the issue will be found in the lunar house. This aspect does not indicate that one's instincts are off base when it comes to karmic awareness, but it does suggest that one may resist inner promptings which stem from the subconscious where memories of the past are stored. If the chart shows negative emotional potentials, these, too, must be corrected.

Natal Moon Opposite Prenatal Eclipse

The conflict described by this opposition is inner conflict rooted in past life failings. On the positive side, the tension displayed here creates a sense of karmic awareness which is almost impossible for the individual to ignore. Upon examining lunar indications in light of other prenatal eclipse findings to determine the exact nature of karmic obligations, one knows the course to follow. It is the individual's responsibility to strive to erase the karmic debts exposed and to strive toward a higher spiritual plane.

Natal Mercury Aspects
to the Prenatal Eclipse

An aspect from Mercury to the prenatal eclipse deals with mental attributes and may pertain to health. It may indicate karmic ties with a sibling or, in some instances, another relative or neighbor.

Natal Mercury Conjunct Prenatal Eclipse

This aspect combines the intellect with prenatal eclipse energies. It requires that the individual not splinter mental energies, that one develop to the fullest natal potential natural mental aptitudes. This conjunction advises that one utilize the reasoning powers and sense of logic available as tools in resolving karmic problems. Notice that Paul's natal Mercury applies to a close conjunction with his prenatal eclipse in Aries in the eleventh house (Figure 6). Tendencies to be hot-headed and mentally impulsive must be overcome if he is to channel the mental energy at his disposal productively and utilize his intellectual resources to further spiritual development.

Natal Mercury Sextile Prenatal Eclipse

The positive mental avenues pointed to by this sextile are karmic assets earned in past lives. The karmic resources identified by Mercury's house position are available for use in resolving karmic issues and helpful in overcoming negative mental attitudes described by Mercury afflictions. It is essential to karmic progress that the Mercury assets not be wasted; to do so compounds karmic debts associated with the prenatal eclipse. This aspect points out opportunities to correctly develop and utilize mental abilities, and this is what one is called upon to do.

Natal Mercury Square Prenatal Eclipse

This square is strongly indicative of inborn mental biases and narrow intellectual concepts that block karmic progress. It serves as a warning flag against prejudicial thinking, unfair decisions, acting on selfish intellectual motives. This aspect is difficult to deal with because the individual is prone to be opinionated. This person feels the need to prove he or she is always right with almost total disregard for the other party's point of view. By overcoming incorrect mental attitudes, one removes a serious barrier to spiritual development.

Natal Mercury Trine Prenatal Eclipse

This aspect indicates that the house occupied by Mercury provides the type of climate which promotes correct mental attitudes and encourages intellectual development. Karmic assets associated with Mercury that one has earned in the past are identified by this trine. The affairs and relationships associated with this aspect are those through which one can work to erase karmic obligations shown by afflictions to the prenatal eclipse. One can look upon Mercury and its attributes as karmic resources waiting to be utilized constructively in the process of spiritual enlightenment.

Natal Mercury Inconjunct Prenatal Eclipse

An inconjunct formed between Mercury and the prenatal eclipse acts as a strong advisory to shape up mentally, to get rid of negative thoughts and unproductive mental attitudes that stand in the way of spiritual growth and karmic progress. If the individual suffers health problems, it is possible they stem from incorrect mental tendencies as described by Mercury in the natal horoscope. In this case, as one develops a spiritually correct mental approach he or she is not only able to deal effectively with karmic issues from the past but health may also improve in the present.

Natal Mercury Opposite Prenatal Eclipse

This opposition produces mental tension which, in turn, can induce one to develop good reasoning powers and the capacity to do his or her own thinking. The person that reacts positively to this aspect can enlarge the scope of intellectual horizons and utilize these abilities to analyze and resolve karmic situations. A negative response frequently results in wishy-washy decision making. The tendency to rely upon popular opinion or the judgment of relatives and acquaintances places another stumbling block in the path of karmic progress.

Natal Venus Aspects
to the Prenatal Eclipse

An aspect between Venus and the prenatal eclipse points to a karmic relationship with a partner, a female relative or friend, or one's lover or spouse. Especially in a man's chart, the wife or sexual partner is apt to be indicated.

Natal Venus Conjunct Prenatal Eclipse

This conjunction joins the love nature with the potential of the prenatal eclipse. Material values associated with Venus are also involved. This aspect emphasizes cooperation, kindness and fair play as inborn attributes to be utilized. If materialistic concerns are shown to be major driving forces, it is imperative that the individual strive to develop the higher Venusian qualities and subdue those that are self- serving. Harmonious social interaction and congenial relationships are important to this individual. A highly afflicted Venus/prenatal eclipse conjunction is indicative of the user; nevertheless, the house of the prenatal eclipse and its affairs are karmic resources to be drawn upon. In the case of an afflicted Venus, it is most important to karmic progress that one strive to overcome the negatives and acquire the positive attitudes and attributes of Venus.

Natal Venus Sextile Prenatal Eclipse

This aspect promotes opportunities for spiritual growth through affairs of the house occupied by Venus and those that Venus governs in the horoscope. One gains satisfaction and support from people connected with these activities. This sextile suggests a warm, friendly climate which induces the individual to reach out and utilize the karmic resources available. Material benefits are also associated with this aspect, benefits which, if shared with society and managed honestly and unselfishly, help promote karmic progress. One has apparently overcome any tendencies toward greed and the acquiring of money for money's sake. Evidently, the individual has learned the lesson of correct stewardship in the past.

Natal Venus Square Prenatal Eclipse

The obstacles pointed to by this square are of a sexual or materialistic nature or both. Gratification through selfish love or the amassing of financial assets endanger one's spiritual growth. The individual may be, in a sense, emotionally isolated from the partner or other close associates by choice, afraid for some deep-seated reason to give too much. A definite lack of warmth in relationships is apparent. With this aspect, one is called upon to learn to put human relationships above material desires and purely sexual needs.

Natal Venus Trine Prenatal Eclipse

This trine fosters the higher qualities of Venus. These attributes as well as the activities and associations described by the house Venus occupies are valuable karmic assets to be utilized in resolving negative karmic issues shown by afflictions to the prenatal eclipse. If the individual takes advantage of the avenues of resource designated by this aspect, he or she can not only erase karmic debts but also gain valuable credits toward the next life. Note that Martin's karmic map (Figure 7) contains a rather wide trine between his key planet, Venusian Gemini in the twelfth house, and his prenatal eclipse in Aquarius in the ninth house. This trine is part of a grand trine that includes natal Pluto in Libra in the fourth house. This configuration points to proper direction of sexual energies (Venus and Pluto) and the evolvement of a correct perspective between material values (Venus) and spiritual values (Pluto), attributes earned in the past that contribute to karmic progress in the present.

Natal Venus Inconjunct Prenatal Eclipse

This aspect gives a solid indication of misuse of sexual energies in past lives. The possibility of prostitution exists. Using sex as a tool for material gain or as a weapon to threaten another person are also possibilities connected with karmic errors. It is essential with this aspect in the chart that one subdue any improper sexual urges and any incorrect material drives that surface. Moreover, it is just as necessary that one strive to develop spiritually correct attitudes and practices in these areas. The activities of the house that Venus occupies may resemble a hotbed of temptation; the relationships described therein are those that entice one into unwise liaisons. For resources that enable the individual to overcome the karmic situation described by this aspect, look to the house of the prenatal eclipse and easy aspects to the prenatal eclipse.

Natal Venus Opposite Prenatal Eclipse

The individual whose horoscope contains this opposition is almost always aware of the conflict between sexual and material desires and spiritual demands. It is that person's karmic responsibility to resolve this conflict in the correct manner. All too frequently, especially in a weak chart, one is trapped by his or her own desires for worldly pleasures and thus compounds karmic debts. One must work to maintain productive relationships that are not disrupted by lack of cooperation or an uncaring attitude on the part of the individual. Too, because of lack of attention, financial affairs connected with the house occupied by Venus may drain other assets.

Natal Mars Aspects
to the Prenatal Eclipse

In general, a Mars aspect to the prenatal eclipse suggests the possibility of karmic links with a male friend or relative.

In a woman's chart. Mars may represent her lover or husband.

Natal Mars Conjunct Prenatal Eclipse

Mars, the dynamic force that it is, energizes prenatal eclipse potentials within the constraints of the sign it occupies. If the conjunction is well aspected, Martian energy can be channeled constructively. In the case of afflictions, one may find it difficult to restrain headstrong and sometimes violent tendencies associated with Mars. The individual may be prodded into plunging headlong into karmic situations with one idea in mind—settle the issue and be done with it one way or the other. Such rash action is often motivated by the desire to do something without even understanding exactly what the issue is all about or the severity of the karmic consequences that can result. Too, with Mars, sexual motivation is always present. One must learn to control the desire nature and harness Mars energy so that it can be directed along positive lines.

Natal Mars Sextile Prenatal Eclipse

This sextile gives positive direction to Martian energies. It offers an opportune setting as described by the house occupied by Mars through which to work out karmic debts. Related activities are productive of spiritual progress; relationships offer the support one needs to do what is necessary to erase karmic debts. The affairs of this house and all that Mars governs in the horoscope as well as the house occupied by the prenatal eclipse are considered karmic resources available to the individual in his or her quest for spiritual growth. This sextile also indicates that one has learned to subdue baser sexual drives, and that the sexual nature has reached a state of near purity, though the individual may not be strong enough not to backslide.

Natal Mars Square Prenatal Eclipse

This square tends to restrain the natural energies of Mars and thus hinder the capacity of Mars as an energizer of the prenatal eclipse. Some people overreact to obstacles in the form of constraints and rebel against the activities and relationships they think confining. This aspect points to a karmic debt that relates to the misuse of Mars energies in past lives. It may refer to belligerence and improper use of physical force, or it may suggest rape or other sexual abuses. In any case, it advises one to redirect initiative and desires toward positive outlets. Mars is a strong motivating factor, and it is important that motivation not be subdued by the pressures associated with this aspect; it is just as important that motivation be channeled into spiritually correct avenues if karmic progress is to be gained.

Natal Mars Trine Prenatal Eclipse

This trine does not weaken the strength of Mars or promote indolence. It does give positive direction to the physical force and sexual desires associated with Mars. Activities and associations found in the house occupied by Mars are assets in the utilization of Martian energies. These are the tools, the karmic resources one has at his or her disposal to utilize in the attempt to erase karmic debts. With this aspect, the path of spiritual progress is eased somewhat as the individual's efforts are usually met with acceptance rather than resistance.

Natal Mars Inconjunct Prenatal Eclipse

This aspect calls for a confrontation, not the usual Mars type confrontation that leads to arguments and sometimes to violence, but a confrontation with one's self. This inconjunct identifies the negative qualities of Mars as karmic offenders, having been misdirected in past lives. The past sexual user and the physical abuser are associated with this aspect. The individual is warned against further abuse. This is a difficult karmic burden, but one that has to be faced up to and in some way atoned for. Here, the prenatal eclipse is the individual's guide to the karmic resources at his or her command. The house occupied by Mars is the place to begin corrective action. It is important that this karmic situation be dealt with properly, as it will remain a serious barrier to karmic progress for many incarnations to come if it is not addressed during the present lifetime.

Natal Mars Opposite Prenatal Eclipse

This opposition pits the physical intensity of Mars against the spiritual energies of the prenatal eclipse. With this aspect, however, one is pulled toward the spiritual. It is advisable to curb resentment at the tug-of-war one is caught up in, to recognize the negative attributes of Mars for what they are and to strive to develop positive qualities. The energy of Mars, when harnessed and directed toward spiritual ends can almost move mountains. No karmic debt is too large to erase with Mars motivation promoting positive action. The key here is, of course, in channeling Mars energies into spiritually productive avenues.

Natal Jupiter Aspects
to the Prenatal Eclipse

Because solar eclipses are based upon the lunation period, they occur at intervals defined by six lunations except during those rare instances when a dual series operates and but one lunation separates two solar eclipses; the succeeding solar eclipse may occur on the fifth following lunation instead of the sixth. Since Jupiter's average motion is less than 15 degrees between six consecutive lunations, if any major aspect is formed with the prenatal eclipse, it is shared by all who were born during the time span in which the aspect was in effect. There are exceptions, however. When Jupiter is direct and in fast motion, it is possible for this planet to form two major aspects within the allowable orb. For example, a square occurring near the date of the appearance of the prenatal eclipse may be followed by a trine in the charts of those born close to the time of the following solar eclipse; some people sharing the same prenatal eclipse might have a square in their chart, others no aspect at all, and yet others could share a trine. By the same token, a trine formed early in the eclipse period might be followed by an inconjunct before the period has expired. As a rule, though, a single aspect between Jupiter and the prenatal eclipse applies to many people. Its general interpretation is to be focalized according to Jupiter's influence in the individual horoscope. In any case, an aspect between Jupiter and the prenatal eclipse usually indicates a past relationship involving the clergy. It always reveals something about moral values and ethics.

Natal Jupiter Conjunct Prenatal Eclipse

This aspect is to be interpreted primarily according to aspects made to the conjunction. A well aspected conjunction is indicative of an inborn sense of proper moral values, an asset to be utilized in all karmic problem areas. An afflicted conjunction points to areas in which immorality could occur; it is the responsibility of the individual to adopt and practice spiritually acceptable standards.

Natal Jupiter Sextile Prenatal Eclipse

People born with this aspect are at a spiritual advantage. This sextile points to correct moral values and an inborn sense of integrity. It offers opportunities for further growth through affairs of the houses occupied and ruled by Jupiter.

Natal Jupiter Square Prenatal Eclipse

This aspect describes karmic obligations created in the past by lack of integrity. It indicates the need to develop proper moral and ethical attitudes. Such action is regarded as a stepping stone to karmic progress. Failure to comply with this karmic directive compounds karmic problems.

Natal Jupiter Trine Prenatal Eclipse

This trine represents karmic resources that are available to the individual. It also represents a group of people who were tested morally at one time or, perhaps, many times; people who succeeded in resisting worldly temptations that offer success at any price, regardless of the method used or concern for who might be hurt on the way.

Natal Jupiter Inconjunct Prenatal Eclipse

The numbers of people who reincarnate under the influence of this aspect represent a group whose sense of integrity is so impaired that they may not be able to distinguish that which is morally right from that which is not. Many simply do not understand what integrity means nor do they comprehend the importance of ethical principles. Usually, one studies Jupiter and its influence in the horoscope to determine how to deal with the problem. If this inconjunct is part of a yod, examine in detail the planet at the focal point for guidance as to how to correct the situation.

Natal Jupiter Opposite Prenatal Eclipse

This opposition alerts one to the necessity of observing spiritually correct moral practices. It also points to activities (the house occupied by and affairs ruled by Jupiter) that are most likely to tempt the individual to commit ethical errors. This aspect serves as a warning signal to all who share it. The penalty for ignoring its message is a barrier to karmic progress, one that the individual will be faced with again in a future incarnation.

Natal Saturn Aspects
to the Prenatal Eclipse

Saturn's average rate of motion during the period between two solar eclipses allows for only one major aspect, if any, to the prenatal eclipse. Interpretation of such an aspect is given a broad connotation unless natal Saturn disposits the prenatal eclipse, is the key planet, the chart ruler or is otherwise prominent in the natal horoscope.

A Saturn aspect to the prenatal eclipse deals with discipline and sense of responsibility. It suggests a karmic relationship with the father figure or other person for whom one has respect. In a woman's chart, it may refer to a karmic tie with her husband.

Natal Saturn Conjunct Prenatal Eclipse

This conjunction implies that one has acquired the discipline and responsibility necessary to carry out directives of the prenatal eclipse. These people take a serious view of their karmic obligations and are well equipped to correctly handle attendant problems.

Natal Saturn Sextile Prenatal Eclipse

Although this sextile does not signify the comfortable setting associated with many other sextiles, it indicates that the affairs of the house occupied by Saturn and the activities this planet governs in the horoscope provide fertile ground for spiritual growth provided that the individual is sincere in his or her efforts. This is not an opportune aspect to be taken for granted. The opportunity to gain karmic progress is open, but the individual must work to achieve the goal.

Natal Saturn Square Prenatal Eclipse

This aspect describes lack of discipline as a major obstacle to karmic progress. In order for one to overcome karmic problems associated with the prenatal eclipse, it is imperative that he or she learn to shoulder responsibility, to resist temptations to take the easy way out. This square often falls in the charts of people who mature late in life, who rely on the parents to take care of them and their problems well into the second Saturn return if family circumstances permit.

Natal Saturn Trine Prenatal Eclipse

This trine is observed in the charts of people who have earned the respect of others in the past for their capacity to shoulder the burdens thrust upon them. This ability is one of their greatest resources in confronting karmic problems. It brings with it a realization of responsibility plus the persistence to carry through with positive action in order to overcome karmic barriers. This aspect in Paul's chart (Figure 6) depicts a solid asset in dealing with prenatal eclipse afflictions.

Natal Saturn Inconjunct Prenatal Eclipse

This is the aspect of the ne'er-do-well and the free loader, the immature. These people have not accepted responsibility in the past and have developed hard-to-break habit patterns that contribute to further karmic debts associated with lack of self-discipline. It is essential with this inconjunct that the individual develop a sense of duty and a serious approach to karmic problems if spiritual growth is to be achieved. Martin's chart (Figure 7) contains this aspect. His need to develop a definite sense of responsibility is further emphasized by the inconjunct from his natal first house Sun to his prenatal eclipse.

Natal Saturn Opposite Prenatal Eclipse

This opposition represents a "let George do it" attitude in which the individual refuses to face up to karmic obligations. He or she may place blame for their problems on anyone except themselves. In order to resolve this dilemma, one must face up to the realities of karmic situations and then act to correct them in a responsible manner.

Natal Uranus Aspects to the Prenatal Eclipse

All persons born with a Uranus/prenatal eclipse aspect share the same aspect. Its personal relevance in the horoscope depends upon Uranus' prominence in the individual chart. Any aspect between natal Uranus and the prenatal eclipse relates to attitudes toward society as a whole and to friends in general. A karmic bond with a friend may be indicated. Uranus/prenatal eclipse aspects are sometimes associated with group karma, group incarnations.

Natal Uranus Conjunct Prenatal Eclipse

This conjunction unites the spirit of brotherly love with potentials of the prenatal eclipse. Here, it is important to keep in mind the essence of universal love as a guiding force in the attempt to erase karmic debts. This aspect reinforces karmic resources described by the prenatal eclipse.

Natal Uranus Sextile Prenatal Eclipse

With this aspect, the house occupied by Uranus and the affairs it governs in the horoscope represent karmic assets. These are the activities and relationships that benefit from one's ingenuity that has been developed in the past and which is a karmic resource to be utilized in the present.

Natal Uranus Square Prenatal Eclipse

This square depicts an uncaring attitude toward humanity, an attitude that stands in the way of karmic progress. People whose horoscopes contain this aspect are not necessarily inhumane, but they are probably indifferent to the needs of society.

It is up to these individuals to generate genuine concern for their fellow human beings. Moreover, the house that contains Uranus points to possible radical activities that must be curbed in the interests of spiritual development. Martin's chart shows that he can look to the Venus (his key planet and ruler of the fifth house which posits Uranus) and Pluto (dispositor of Uranus) trines to his prenatal eclipse for the means of overcoming the implications of this square.

Natal Uranus Trine Prenatal Eclipse

With this aspect, the individual's friends and colleagues serve as bridges that span the breaks between karmic problems and spiritually correct solutions. Relationships are important here as karmic resources. It is with the support and assistance of these people that one can overcome karmic barriers and advance on the karmic wheel.

Natal Uranus Inconjunct Prenatal Eclipse

This aspect describes fanatical tendencies that must be subdued. It also points to spiritually incorrect social attitudes and calls upon one to examine his or her role as a social force. This aspect is frequently seen in the charts of misguided activists. It is essential that one accept the proper role in society and not espouse anarchy or other causes whose sole purpose is to destroy. Positive change is a goal worth striving for, but one needs to examine the motives behind such change in order to choose the course that leads to karmic progress. In Paul's chart, with Uranus in the sixth house inconjunct both Mercury and the prenatal eclipse, karmic related health problems may also be indicated.

Natal Uranus Opposite Prenatal Eclipse

This opposition is the aspect of the rebel without a cause. These people tend to stir up trouble when none exists. It is important that one channel Uranian energy into spiritually acceptable avenues. This is a high energy aspect, and one can accomplish much if energies are utilized to resolve karmic situations and not thrust into activities that are irresponsible in relation to the karmic plateau.

Natal Neptune Aspects to the Prenatal Eclipse

Neptune, the upper octave of Venus, brings the love nature to the higher spiritual plateau. Since Neptune moves so slowly during the interim between two solar eclipses, it will either form no aspect with a common prenatal eclipse, or it will form one aspect shared by many of those born under that particular prenatal eclipse.

Natal Neptune Conjunct Prenatal Eclipse

In order to determine the essence of this aspect, other aspects to the conjunction must be analyzed. A Neptune/prenatal eclipse conjunction that is well aspected brings one's spiritual resources to the fore, to be utilized according to the course pointed out in the horoscope. However, if the conjunction is afflicted, one may be blind to the message of the prenatal eclipse, or at the very least will probably misconstrue its direction. Many of these people join cults in search of spiritual growth, following as sheep in a herd to an inevitable karmic stalemate rather than pursuing the path of karmic progress charted m their horoscope.

Natal Neptune Sextile Prenatal Eclipse

This sextile offers opportunities for spiritual development through the relationships and affairs associated with Neptune and the prenatal eclipse. Here, the more lofty side of Neptune's nature emerges. One's spiritual and psychic powers, one's sensitivity and compassion are among karmic resources available to the individual. This aspect is indicative of circumstances that encourage one to use his or her positive Neptunian attributes.

Natal Neptune Square Prenatal Eclipse

This aspect describes the escapist, one who has resorted to alcohol, drugs, an imaginary world or other means to escape reality in past lives. Too, there may be inborn fraudulent tendencies present. This square warns against deception and chicanery. It requires that one resist Neptunian temptations and build character traits based upon realism and honesty if karmic debts are to be erased. The house occupied by Neptune and the affairs the planet governs represent sources of difficulty; they can be worked out through directions prescribed by the prenatal eclipse.

Natal Neptune Trine Prenatal Eclipse

This trine provides an easy flow of spiritual energy between Neptune and affairs of the prenatal eclipse. The house occupied by Neptune is a resource house which can be utilized to work out karmic obligations shown by afflictions to the prenatal eclipse. Neptune's house and all that it governs in the horoscope supplement resources described by the prenatal eclipse. This aspect occurs in the horoscopes of people who are at a high level on the karmic wheel. This aspect is reinforced in Paul's chart as it is part of a grand trine that includes natal Saturn and the prenatal eclipse.

Natal Neptune Inconjunct Prenatal Eclipse

This aspect calls attention to the misuse of positive Neptunian energies in the past and urges that one comply with prenatal eclipse directives if that person is not to be left to flounder on the karmic wheel. People with this inconjunct in their horoscope have had opportunities in past lives to grow spiritually, but have failed to do so because they have succumbed to drugs or other escapist temptations and in so doing have amassed karmic debts. It is essential that the individual face reality and accept his or her karmic responsibility in order to develop spiritually correct characteristics.

Natal Neptune Opposite Prenatal Eclipse

The tension associated with this opposition usually does not create the awareness displayed by oppositions formed between the prenatal eclipse and other planets. Instead, confusion and chaos may result as the individual is pulled between reality and illusion, between truth and fallacy. One may be prone to self-delusion, or he or she may be the victim or perpetrator of deception. It is important that this aspect be analyzed with utmost objectivity if one is to comprehend the nature of related karmic situations. It is essential if karmic progress is to be achieved that one not follow the escapist route. This aspect signals the need to approach karmic issues sensibly and realistically.

Natal Pluto Aspects
to the Prenatal Eclipse

Pluto aspects describe evolution on the spiritual level. They describe the metamorphosis of the entity called soul. The very nature of this planet calls attention to the loftiest spiritual aspirations as well as to the most debasing attributes of humankind. It brings with it the realization that humanity has a spiritual and an animal nature. Generally, no aspect or but one aspect is formed by Pluto with a particular prenatal eclipse, an aspect shared by the majority of people who share that prenatal eclipse.

Natal Pluto Conjunct Prenatal Eclipse

This aspect describes a group of people who have reincarnated during a period in which Pluto is influential. The nature of this aspect calls for unification of Plutonian energies with those of the prenatal eclipse. This is a power aspect, and the individual's response is the key to karmic growth or, in the case of a negative reaction resulting in misuse of energies, serious karmic setbacks. A negative response reflects gang wars, rape and other criminal offenses. A positive response generates the power of a charismatic leader of the masses.

Natal Pluto Sextile Prenatal Eclipse

This sextile offers a climate that nourishes spiritual growth. Karmic assets are found in the house Pluto occupies and the activities and relationships it governs in the horoscope. The people who share this aspect are among those who have reached a high degree of spiritual evolvement. They have the opportunity through Pluto's regenerative attributes of paying off karmic debts described by afflictions to the prenatal eclipse and thereby gaining much progress on the karmic wheel.

Natal Pluto Square Prenatal Eclipse

The strictures associated with this square are those associated with ruthless behavior and criminal tendencies stemming from brutal pastlife experiences. If other elements in the horoscope agree, the individual may feel overwhelmed by cruel urges which he or she does not understand, but often finds difficult to resist. Sometimes children too young to know the harm of the deed display a propensity to torture animals. Here, it is important that they receive guidance so that they learn at a young age how to redirect this energy along positive lines. Once the obstacles of the square are overcome, the individual can proceed to deal with other karmic issues.

Natal Pluto Trine Prenatal Eclipse

This is the aspect of the enlightened ones, those who have in the past gained deep spiritual understanding. These people naturally draw upon Plutonian energies in the process of karmic evolvement. Martin's horoscope contains just such a trine, part of a grand trine involving his key planet, Venus, and the prenatal eclipse. Although his chart contains the difficult Uranus square to his prenatal eclipse plus the karmic yod involving the Sun, Saturn and the prenatal eclipse, he has the spiritual assets at hand to effectively deal with karmic issues and erase karmic debts accrued in the past. Anyone whose chart displays this aspect has a strong bent toward spiritual ends and the resources with which to resolve karmic barriers.

Natal Pluto Inconjunct Prenatal Eclipse

This inconjunct points to serious karmic offenses often of a vicious nature committed in the past. These people may be on a such a merry-go-round of brutality that they have no conception of right and wrong. This aspect is not one to take lightly. The prenatal eclipse and its affairs as well as the easy aspects it forms all point to karmic resources through which one can re-direct negative Plutonian attributes acquired in past lives into spiritually acceptable avenues. If this inconjunct completes a yod the natal horoscope, the connecting sextile is a reliable guide as to how to properly address the karmic aspects of the situation.

Natal Pluto Opposite Prenatal Eclipse

This aspect does not indicate lack of spiritual development, but it does indicate a critical point in karmic evolvement. The individual faces a choice between striving for higher attainments on the spiritual plane or reverting to the animalism of the earthly plane. Paul's natal Pluto opposes his prenatal eclipse which is fairly well aspected. His chart clearly indicates that he not only has awareness of his karmic responsibilities, created by the opposition, but also has the karmic resources at his disposal to meet the demands of the Uranus/prenatal eclipse inconjunct.

Aspects Between the Horizontal Angles of the Horoscope and the Prenatal Eclipse

When the prenatal eclipse is in aspect with the Ascendant of a horoscope, it also forms a complementary aspect with the Descendant. These aspects combine personal qualities described by the Ascendant with one's capacity to relate to others on a one-to-one basis as indicated by the Descendant. The meanings given must be adapted to accommodate expression described by the signs on the angles. Martin's prenatal eclipse does not aspect the horizontal angles. Paul's forms only minor aspects, a semisquare to the Ascendant complemented by a sesquiquadrate to the Descendant. These aspects suggest that Paul may take too lightly (a Gemini quality) thoughtless personal acts that detract from the quality of seventh house relationships. With Sagittarius on the Descendant and Neptune occupying the natal seventh house, he may be looking for the "ideal" partner with no strings attached. This is one facet of his personality, though not a serious one in terms of karmic responsibility, that he should work on in order to perfect personal characteristics and his attitude in relating to others.

Natal Ascendant Conjunct and
Natal Descendant Opposite Prenatal Eclipse

These aspects place responsibility for resolving karmic debts directly upon the individual. They arouse a sense of self-direction. It is important that the individual strive to develop positive attributes of the Ascendant and first house. To do so enables that person to reach out to fulfilling relationships. Not to do so encourages discord in marriage and conflict in business partnerships. However, both houses, the first and the seventh, can be considered resource houses if the individual utilizes them in spiritually correct ways. If the prenatal eclipse falls in the twelfth house instead of the first, these aspects may point to psychological problems or congenital physical defects rooted in past karmic errors.

Natal Ascendant Sextile and
Natal Descendant Trine Prenatal Eclipse

Individuals whose charts contain these aspects have reached a high level of self-understanding and consideration for others. Self-acceptance and the capacity to establish productive relationships are among their karmic assets. Karmic problems described by afflictions to the prenatal eclipse can be worked out through personal efforts as well as those of their chosen counterpart.

Natal Ascendant and Natal
Descendant Square Prenatal Eclipse

These aspects place the prenatal eclipse at the focal point of a T-square. Karmic obligations stemming from selfish personal tendencies and inconsiderate treatment of partners in past lives must be addressed through the house of the prenatal eclipse and the resources described by its easy aspects. Failure to heed prenatal eclipse directives stunts the personality and inhibits the capacity to form satisfying relationships. Here, character development becomes an important part of spiritual growth.

Natal Ascendant Trine and Natal
Descendant Sextile Prenatal Eclipse

These aspects indicate a highly evolved personality and point to beneficial seventh house relationships as support groups which encourage spiritual enlightenment. Frequently the spouse is instrumental in helping the individual effectively deal with karmic problems, although recognition of such problems usually comes about through the individual's inborn sense of self-awareness.

Natal Ascendant Inconjunct and Natal Descendant Semisextile Prenatal Eclipse

The individual in whose horoscope these aspects appear has apparently long trodden a path of self-interest with little concern for the needs of others. If the prenatal eclipse is highly afflicted, exploitation of others for personal gain in the past may be indicated. One must examine the motives behind his or her actions and uncover those which are purely selfish. Only by subduing ingrained self-centered traits can this individual earn the karmic credits necessary to proceed further along the path to spiritual evolvement. If the complementary aspect to the Descendant, a minor one, is within the two degree allowable orb, seventh house activities and relationships offer some support for spiritual development.

Natal Descendant Inconjunct and Natal Ascendant Semisextile Prenatal Eclipse

The inconjunct here refers to lack of fairness in treatment of those with whom one was closely associated in the past and demands that one develop concern for the needs of others. Lack of cooperation oa the part of the individual or the inability to relate to spouse or partners impedes karmic progress. If the minor complementary aspect to the Ascendant is within orb, the individual may possess innate character traits upon which to draw that enable him to realize his or her karmic obligations. Whether or not the semisextile to the Ascendant is valid, the burden of developing spiritually healthy seventh house attitudes is upon the individual.

Natal Ascendant Opposite and Natal Descendant Conjunct Prenatal Eclipse

With these aspects it is important to karmic progress that the individual maintain supportive seventh house relationships, for they represent strong karmic assets. One's personal growth plays an important part in spiritual progress, and it is through seventh house affairs that one can learn the lessons of spiritually correct character development, lessons that promote karmic evolvement.

Aspects Between the Vertical Angles of the Horoscope and the Prenatal Eclipse

An aspect between the Midheaven (MC) and the prenatal eclipse focuses on worldly ambitions; its complimentary aspect with the *imum coeli* (IC), sometimes incorrectly referred to as the Nadir of the horoscope, draws in family concerns. These aspects stress the fact that one cannot completely separate domestic affairs from outside interests. Activity in the area of the horoscope influenced by the Midheaven also affects those associated with the *imum coeli* and vice versa.

Natal MC Conjunct and Natal MC Opposite Prenatal Eclipse

These aspects are indicative of an inborn power drive, the desire to achieve a degree of greatness in keeping with potentials of the natal horoscope. If the prenatal eclipse is heavily afflicted, the individual has probably misused his or her worldly position for selfish ends in the past. It is important not to repeat this karmic error in the present. The individual can look upon the fourth house and the activities and relationships it describes as karmic resources. Because the focus is on the tenth house by virtue of the MC/prenatal eclipse conjunction, the individual may fail to utilize fourth house assets even though the opposition creates a sense of awareness. If the prenatal eclipse falls in the ninth instead of the tenth, greater spiritual motivation is present.

Natal MC Sextile and Natal IC Trine Prenatal Eclipse

The public life and the career setting offer opportunities for spiritual growth when these aspects appear in the horoscope.

In all likelihood, the parents have provided the type of child-hood that lends support to the individual throughout the present lifetime. These aspects call for one to use whatever worldly influence they have at their disposal as a positive example of spiritually correct action and thus obliterate karmic debts acquired in the past. Paul's chart contains these aspects which are supplemented by the trine from natal Saturn, natural ruler of the tenth house posited in the fourth, to his prenatal eclipse. These aspects give guidance as to how Paul can deal with the inconjunct between his prenatal eclipse and Uranus, ruler of his Midheaven.

Natal MC and Natal IC Square Prenatal Eclipse

These squares are associated with an inborn "success at any price" attitude, an attitude that blocks karmic progress and, if allowed to remain unchecked, one that can compound karmic debts. The individual may have little respect for home and family. The urge to act like a big shot to try to prove to world the extent of one's capabilities may be present. The acquiring of humility, appreciation of the value of family life and positive attitudes toward the use of worldly influence are worthy spiritual goals. With this combination of aspects, the prenatal eclipse falls at the focal point of a T-square. It is through the karmic resources found at this focal point that one must work in order to overcome obstacles associated with the vertical angles in order to achieve karmic progress.

Natal MC Trine and Natal IC Sextile Prenatal Eclipse

The individual whose horoscope contains these aspects has earned a niche in the world by contributing his or her efforts to making the world a better place in which to live. Selfish ambition has been conquered, and this person recognizes the value of his or her heritage. Tenth and fourth house interests combine to further karmic advances as described by the prenatal eclipse.

Natal MC Inconjunct and Natal
IC Semisextile Prenatal Eclipse

These aspects call for a definite change of direction in regard to one's approach to worldly objectives. The time to reevaluate worldly goals is now. The inconjunct is frequently found in the horoscopes of those who were so driven toward success and prestige in past lives that they trampled on whomever had the misfortune to be in their way. The lessons to be learned here may be difficult and often involve the downfall of a successful person who has placed worldly gains above spiritually correct behavior. The individual who recognizes and deals with the karmic error may go far in this world as well as advance on the karmic wheel. Success per se is not the important issue, it is one's perception of success that counts. If the IC/semisextile is within orb, one can depend on the guidance and support of parents.

Natal IC Inconjunct and Natal
MC Semisextile Prenatal Eclipse

The karmic focus with these aspects lies in the fourth house. No doubt karmic debts have occurred in the past as a result of parental neglect, a selfish attitude toward family members or the tendency to dominate the home. It is imperative that the individual not repeat these mistakes, that he or she develop proper family attitudes and a sense of responsibility toward home and family affairs. If an MC/prenatal eclipse occurs in connection with the inconjunct, the tenth house can be looked upon as spiritually supportive in nature.

Natal MC Opposite and Natal
IC Conjunct Prenatal Eclipse

These aspects alert one of the karmic hazards of wrongful actions that not only attract the attention of the public but may also influence others to follow in the same footsteps. This aspect may be found in the horoscopes of the famous who, instead of being role models for their fellow human beings, follow a course of decadence and thus sway others toward a path of degeneration. It is important that the individual live an exemplary public life, that he or she strives to be a strong force in lighting the way to spiritual growth. Here, the fourth house and the relationships and activities with which it is associated represent karmic assets available to the individual.

Chapter 6

Progressed and Transiting Aspects to the Prenatal Eclipse

The prenatal eclipse, accompanying lunar eclipse and the initial eclipse do not progress; they are points in the horoscope that remain in place throughout one's lifetime. As other elements of the natal horoscope progress, however, planets which did or did not aspect the prenatal eclipse natally may form progressed aspects with it, thus activating dormant potentials and further defining the scope of prenatal eclipse influence.

These progressed aspects describe unfolding growth patterns, opportunities for karmic progress and lessons yet to be learned according to the nature of the aspect and the planet involved. Even if the progressed planet does not form a natal aspect with the prenatal eclipse, some astrological relationship between the two will be found to tie in the natal promise of the prenatal eclipse with that planet. For example, Paul's natal Mars, which makes no natal aspect with his prenatal eclipse, will progress to a trine with his prenatal eclipse when he is about 26 years old. Mars disposits his prenatal eclipse in Aries, thus forming a natal connection.

The heavier planets progress so slowly that they seldom

do more than close an applying natal aspect or move out of orb of a separating aspect. For example, the applying natal Saturn/prenatal eclipse inconjunct in Martin's horoscope will progress to partile in his 38th year and will remain within natal orb for more than 100 years, much longer than the average lifespan. Yet, his natal Neptune which lacks just 27 minutes of being in natal orb of a sextile with his prenatal eclipse will not form a progressed sextile (one degree orb) in this lifetime.

In any case, an aspect from a progressed planet or major transit to the initial eclipse or to a planet in natal aspect with the prenatal eclipse will activate natal prenatal eclipse potentials even though the orb may be too wide to include the prenatal eclipse. With the exception of transiting solar and lunar eclipses, the orb for all progressed and transiting aspects is one degree, and the period of influence covers the entire time during which the aspect remains within the allowable orb. The usual orb for transiting eclipses is five degrees; the tighter the orb, the stronger the effect of the aspect. The period of influence extends until the succeeding eclipse sequence occurs in about six months. In the event a transiting solar eclipse forms a close conjunction with the prenatal eclipse, within 2°30' of partile, the aspect is interpreted as a return; its period of influence is one year.

Prenatal Eclipse Returns

The majority of solar eclipses, about 75 percent, observe a Metonic return, recurring in approximately the same zodiacal position at 19 year intervals. A prenatal eclipse return represents an important period in life and, perhaps, a critical one. It may mark a major milestone or turning point, although its impact frequently is not immediately apparent.

Martin's prenatal eclipse, which follows the Metonic pattern of regularity, will return in February 16, 1999. Considering his age at that time, just five months short of 19, and the fact that his prenatal eclipse is posited in his natal ninth house, 1999 may be a crucial year for him in terms of his college education.

Paul's prenatal eclipse does not follow a regular return. Its first return occurred on April 9,1986, two weeks prior to his eighth birthday. At the time, Paul was not doing well in school. His lack of interest was compounded by the fact that he disliked his teacher who was, in his words, "a mean old witch." As the summer progressed, his interest in canoeing and fishing developed and at this writing he is skilled in both sports. Through these activities, he met a lad his own age with whom he could relate. They became and still are best friends. One cannot say what turned his interest in school around, but he is presently a good student and popular with his peers (eleventh house prenatal eclipse).

Some returns have greater significance, although their influence cannot be judged at the time. For example, John F. Kennedy experienced an early prenatal eclipse return in 1925, the year his brother Robert was born. No one can doubt the influence Robert had in John's political career, although at the time it is unlikely that anyone could have been aware of the implications. Thereafter, John Kennedy's prenatal eclipse recurred with Metonic regularity. It appeared in 1944, the year his older brother, Joseph, was killed. Joseph's death served as a turning point in John's life, for his own presidential aspirations stemmed from that event. It is common knowledge that Joseph was being groomed for the presidency, and upon his death, the second eldest Kennedy son stepped into Joseph's political shoes. John's final prenatal eclipse return occurred in 1963, ten months prior to his assassination. John Kennedy's horoscope is shown in Chapter 7.

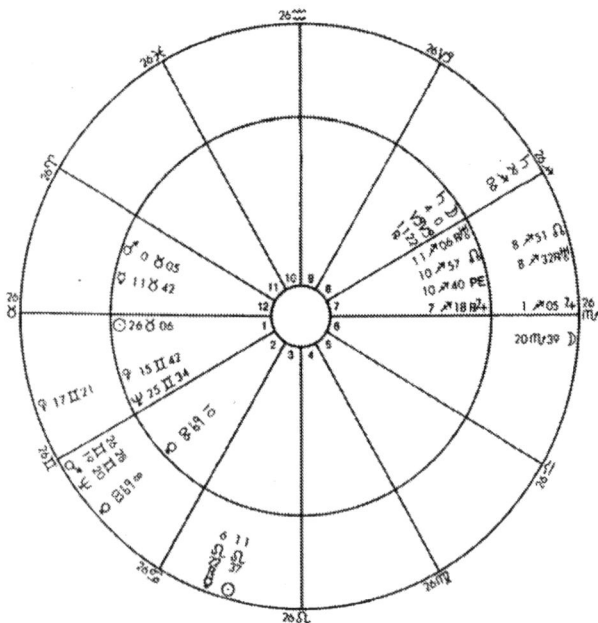

May 17, 1900
Solar chart progressed to the year
his forces seized power in Iran.

Figure 8   The Ayatollah Ruhollah Khomeini

Prenatal Eclipse Related Events

A progressed aspect to the prenatal eclipse that remains in
force for more than a year, which all do except those formed by
the progressed Moon, describes a developmental period that is
part of the overall evolution associated with the prenatal
eclipse. It may also suggest various events. An exact hard aspect (one degree orb), major or minor, by the progressed Moon
or a transiting planet usually times a karmic event that occurs
during the period. For instance, the solar chart of the Ayatollah
Khomeini (Figure 8) shows that his progressed Sun in Leo was
separating from a trine with his prenatal eclipse in 10 Sagittarius 40, though still within orb at the time of the Khomeini takeover in Iran on February 11, 1979. Natally, the Sun and prena-

tal eclipse are not in aspect, but the Sun's dispositor, Venus (10 Cancer), forms an exact inconjunct with the prenatal eclipse and exactly sextiles the initial eclipse in 10 Taurus which Venus also disposits. On the morning of the takeover, the transiting Moon (dispositor of natal Venus) squared the initial eclipse and formed a partile conjunction with the progressed Sun to trigger action. Some of the problems that lie ahead for the first few weeks can be described by transiting Saturn, retrograde, which moved into orb of a square with the prenatal eclipse within four days of the takeover.

Progressed and transiting aspects that influence the prenatal eclipse are interpreted according to the nature of the aspect and the planet involved. That planet's influence in the individual's horoscope must also be considered. The faster moving transits usually do not have much significance other than to trigger an event whose potential is already shown in the chart natally or by progression. The heavier transits whose aspects remain in orb for a period of weeks or months have more influence as do transiting eclipses.

The lunar eclipse in 3 Aquarius 12 that preceded John F. Kennedy's September 1953 marriage to Jacqueline Bouvier (Figure 12) was conjunct his prenatal eclipse in 2 Aquarius 45. The morning of his wedding day, the transiting Moon squared the eclipse point to activate potentials and transiting Mars, ruler of his natal seventh house, was conjunct his initial eclipse in 28 Leo. Coincidentally, the solar eclipse in 16 Leo 45 that preceded the marriage squared Jacqueline's prenatal eclipse in 18 Taurus 08 and, on the day of the wedding, transiting Venus (dispositor other prenatal eclipse and ruler other natal seventh house) was conjunct the eclipse point.

Chapter 7

Relationships from the Past to the Present

An aspect from one person's prenatal eclipse to a point in another person's horoscope represents a karmic link, one that implies the two have had some contact in a past life, with exact major aspects, including the inconjunct, carrying the most weight in terms of karmic debts and assets.

Squares, inconjuncts and oppositions describe karmic debts owed by the person whose prenatal eclipse aspects another's chart, a debt owed to the other person. If both prenatal eclipses form a major hard aspect in each other's charts, mutual karmic debts are implied. Trines and sextiles are not associated with karmic debts; they suggest a prior relationship in which debts have been cleared. They are considered karmic assets which are supportive in nature. A conjunction is interpreted according to the nature of the planet involved; it indicates the need to unify.

The closer the aspect, the stronger the karmic tie. Although an orb of up to five degrees is allowable for major aspects between charts, exact aspects (1 degree orb) are those most commonly found linking charts of people who have great impact on each other's lives. For this reason, examples in this chapter consider primarily only exact prenatal eclipse aspects. Wider aspects, especially those with orbs greater than two degrees, suggest a casual association such as one might establish with a supermarket clerk or bank teller. You are acquainted with each other but know little about one another's personal life. Exact aspects link the charts of married couples, lovers, parents and children or, perhaps, that of a teacher and student whose relationship is meaningful. The relationship shown in the charts may refer to a past life association or to one established in the present or both.

Prenatal Eclipse Ties

For example, upon comparing Paul's chart with Martin's (Figures 1 and 3), one sees that Paul's prenatal eclipse in 17 Aries 27 forms an exact opposition with Martin's natal Moon in the natal fourth house of Martin's horoscope. It also forms a wider sextile with Martin's natal Venus, his key planet, and an opposition with Martin's natal Pluto. The orb of both these aspects is under two degrees. By themselves, they would not indicate a strong and meaningful relationship. The lunar opposition suggests that Martin may have been Paul's mother in a prior lifetime. Martin's key planet, Venus, indicates that he was a female in a former incarnation and Paul's natal chart suggests a parental relationship as part of his karmic heritage. Note that Martin's prenatal eclipse in 26 Aquarius 50 forms no exact aspects in Paul's chart, with his prenatal eclipse square to Paul's natal Venus being the closest aspect with 1° 27' orb. These aspects indicate that the relationship is a bit one-sided, with Paul owing the karmic debt to Martin as described by the exact lunar/prenatal eclipse opposition. Being a separative aspect, the opposition implies that Paul has had a serious break with Martin in the past that now needs mending. Whatever their relationship in a past life, they are first cousins in this one.

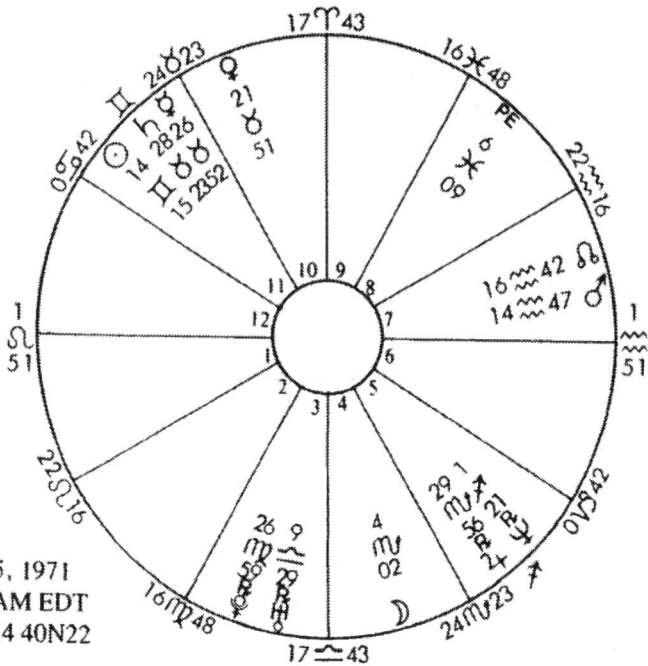

Figure 9 Natal Horoscope for Eddy

It is interesting to note that Martin and his older brother. Eddy, share mutual prenatal eclipse ties (Figure 9). Martin's prenatal eclipse forms an exact square with Eddy's natal Mercury, within two minutes of partile, and an exact trine with Eddy's natal Pluto, posited in the natal third house, suggesting a sibling relationship. Eddy's prenatal eclipse in 6 Pisces 09 forms an exact trine with Martin's Ascendant. Eddy's prenatal eclipse forms no exact aspects with Paul's chart, though the trine to Paul's natal Moon would suggest a prior association. No doubt that Eddy will play a part in Martin's karmic progress, but he owes no karmic debt to Martin. His is a supportive role and, with Martin's Ascendant involved, one that contributes to Martin's personal development.

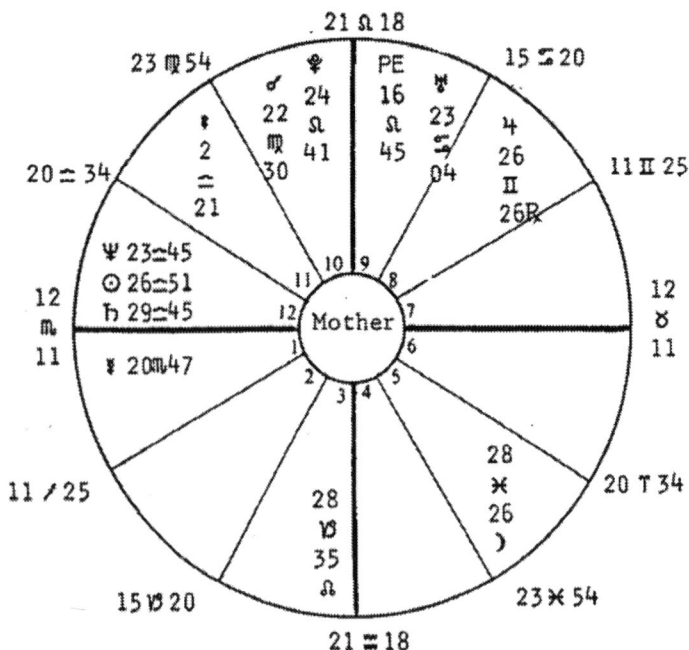

Figure 10   Horoscopes of the Smith Family

A Karmic Bridge

Infrequently, one person's prenatal eclipse will aspect another person's, both of which aspect a third party's horoscope. A common prenatal eclipse aspect acts as a karmic bridge which brings the two together in order to work out karmic obligations with a third person. The horoscopes of Mrs. Smith and her son (Figure 10) show just such a karmic bridge.

Her prenatal eclipse in 16 Leo 45 forms an exact inconjunct with her child's prenatal eclipse in 16 Pisces 44. No other major exact prenatal eclipse aspects link the two charts; both are linked to the horoscope of the father and vice versa. His prenatal eclipse in 27 Leo 31 forms an exact sextile with her natal Sun and an inconjunct with her natal Moon, It inconjuncts her

96

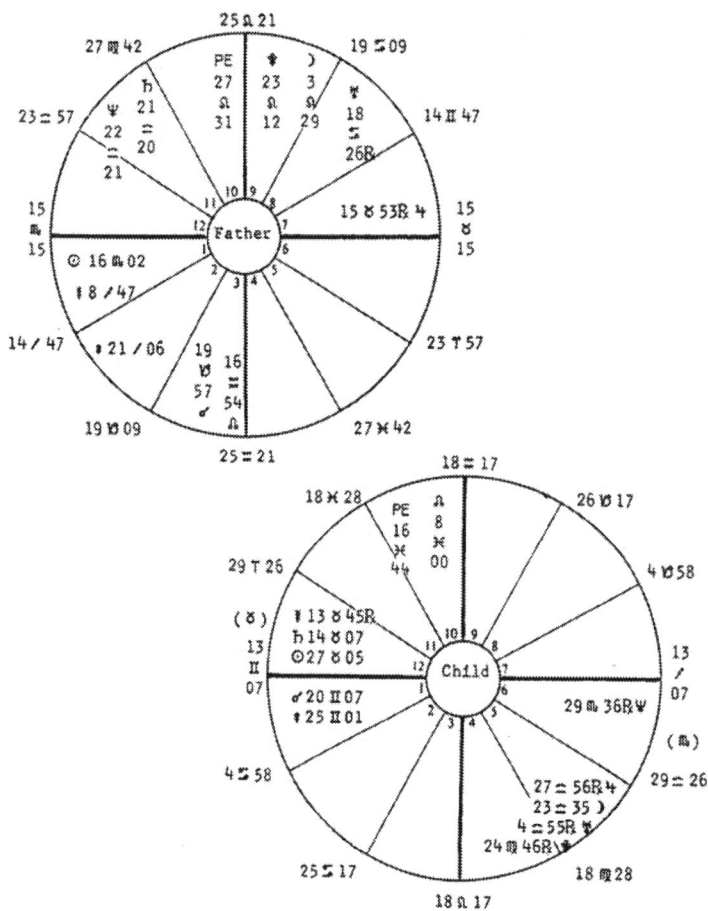

Father's Chart

25 Ω 21

27 ♍ 42

19 ♋ 09

PE 27 Ω 31 ☿ 23 Ω 12 ☽ 3 Ω 29

♅ 18 ♋ 26R

♄ 21 ♎ 20

♆ 22 ♎ 21

23 ♎ 57

14 ♊ 47

15 ♏

15 ♉ 53R ♃

15 ♉ 15

⊙ 16 ♏ 02

♇ 8 ♐ 47

14 ♐ 47

♂ 21 ♐ 06

19 ♑ 57 ♀ 16 ♒ 54 ☊

23 ♈ 57

19 ♑ 09

27 ♓ 42

25 ♒ 21

Father

Child's Chart

18 ♎ 17

18 ♓ 28

26 ♑ 17

PE 16 ♓ 00 ☊ 8 ♓ ♃

29 ♈ 26

4 ♑ 58

(♉) 13 ♊ 07

♇ 13 ♉ 45R ♄ 14 ♉ 07 ⊙ 27 ♉ 05

13 ♐ 07

♂ 20 ♊ 07 ♀ 25 ♊ 01

29 ♏ 36R ♆

4 ♋ 58

(♏) 29 ♎ 26

27 ♎ 56R ♃ 23 ♎ 35 ☽ 4 ♎ 55R ♅ 24 ♏ 46R ☿

18 ♍ 28

25 ♋ 17

18 Ω 17

Child

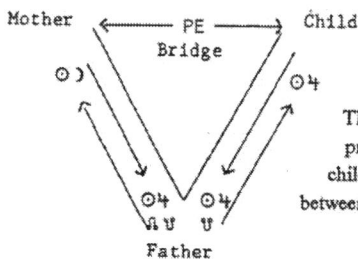

The bridge in the diagram represents the prenatal eclipse between the mother and child. Arrows indicate exact major aspects between the prenatal eclipse in one horoscope and planets in the others.

Figure 10   Horoscopes of the Smith Family

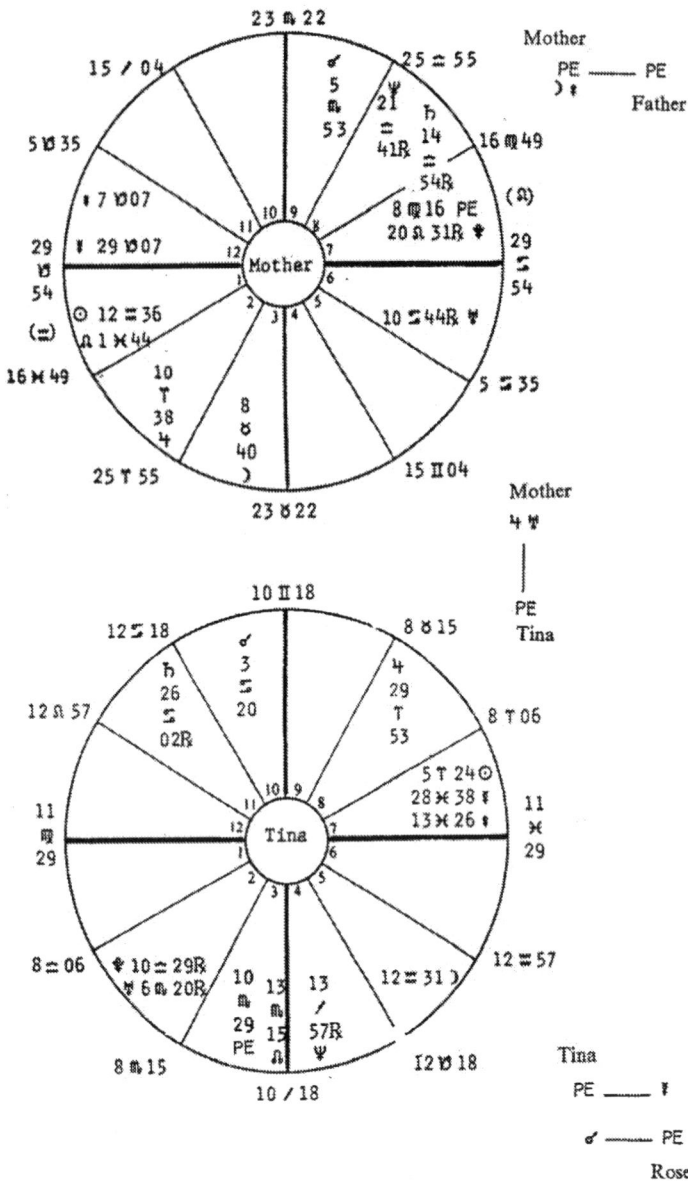

Figure 11   Prenatal Eclipse Ties

Father chart

20 ♓ 39

26 ♈ 15

(♉)

PE 7 ♉ 42

♈ 16

6 ♊ 09

23 ♒ 07

1 ♒ 06

♈ 4 ♎ 55

22 ♑ 26 ♃

12 ♎ 04

10 9
11   8
12 Father 7
1   6
2   5
3 4

12 ♑ 04

1 ♌ 06

24 ♏

11 ♌ 48

17 ♌ 32

13 ♏ 03 ☽

6 ♐ 09

(♏)

12 ♍ 32 ♄

2 ♎ 45 ⊙

14 ♎ 28 ♆

17 ♎ 39R ♀

26 ♎ 15

Father ⊙

PE Rose

23 ♌ 07

20 ♍ 39

Rose chart

27 ♈ 29

(♉)

4 ♊ 07

25 ♓ 40

9 ♋ 25

♄ 27 ♊ 49R

♂ 26 ♉ 26

9 ♓ 43R ♀
1 ♓ 51 ⊙

0 ♓ 19

9 ♌ 34

10 9
11   8
12 Rose 7
1   6
2   5
3 4

26 ♒ 18 ♃
16 ♒ 45 ☽

9 ♒ 34

0 ♍ 19

26 ♑ 54 ♀

9 ♑ 25

6 ♎ 20R ♇

27 ♎ 36R ♅

2 ♑ 40 PE
26 ♐ 30 ♌
9 ♐ 31 ♆

4 ♐ 07

25 ♍ 40

27 ♎ 29 (♏)

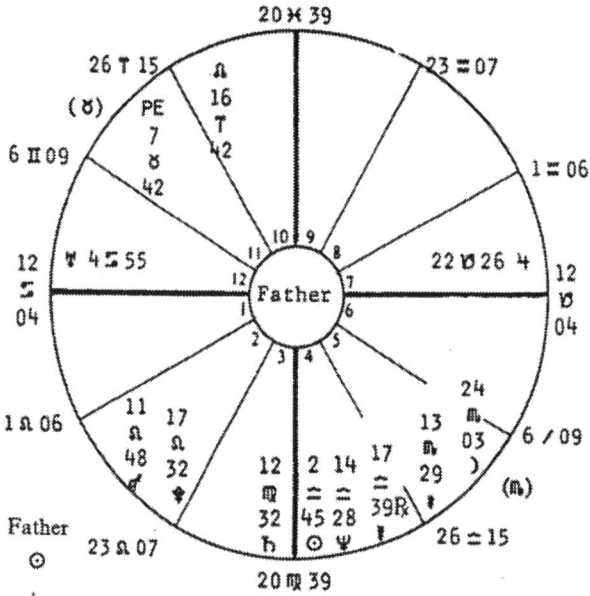

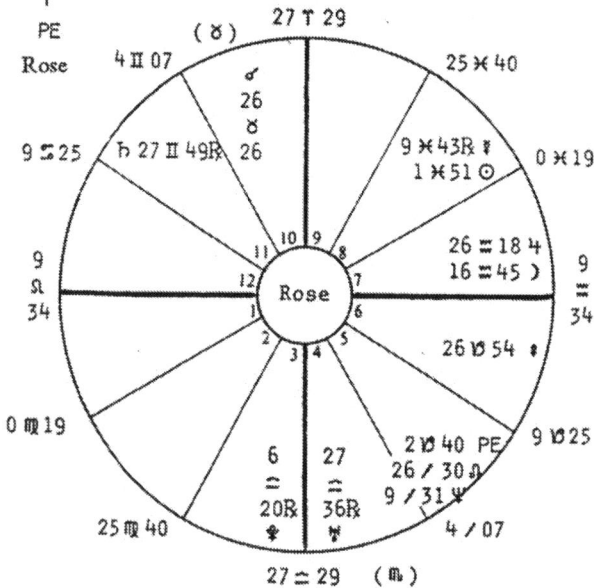

Figure 11A   Prenatal Eclipse Ties

North Node and squares her natal Jupiter just minutes short of exactness. It also exactly squares the child's natal Sun and sextiles his natal Jupiter. The mother's prenatal eclipse squares the father's natal Sun and Jupiter and conjuncts his South Node. The child's prenatal eclipse trines the father's natal Sun, sextiles his natal Jupiter and forms an inconjunct with the South Node, all exact aspects. The parents share mutual eclipse ties and so do the father and child. Usually, a karmic bridge is found in the charts of parents' horoscopes who bring a third person into the world, their child, with whom both share karmic obligations. In this instance, though, the child formed the bridge with the mother, and the two brought the father into their life. She was pregnant before she married, though the boy was born after the wedding.

Family Connections

Not all members of the same earthly family share exact prenatal eclipse ties. One member may share with another and not with the others.

The charts of Tina and Rose, sisters, show that they share karmic ties with each other. Tina's prenatal eclipse in 10 Scorpio 29 trines her sister's natal Mercury, ruler of the natal third house. It also forms two exact aspects in her mother's chart, an inconjunct to natal Jupiter and a trine to natal Uranus. It forms no exact aspects in her father's chart, nor does his prenatal eclipse in 7 Taurus 42 form an exact aspect in hers. Rose's prenatal eclipse in 2 Capricorn 40 trines her sister's natal Mars, ruler of her third house and squares her father's natal Sun; it forms no exact aspect with her mother's chart. Although the parent's prenatal eclipses form a bridge and the father's prenatal eclipse aspects the mother's chart, neither of their prenatal eclipses forms an exact aspect in either child's chart, close but not exact. It is clear that Tina's obligations to her mother and

Rose's to her father are one-sided, with each child indebted to one parent. It would seem that the parents reincarnated to provide a setting in which the children could work out their mutual obligations with each other and their individual responsibilities to a parent.

Some family karmic relationships are extremely complex. The family of Rose and Joseph P. Kennedy, Sr. are a prime example of interwoven karmic relationships. Their collective horoscopes contain innumerable prenatal eclipse ties. Their charts are shown and karmic links tabulated in my *Eclipses: Astrological Guideposts*.

One-time Encounters

Have you ever met a stranger with whom you immediately felt comfortable and sensed that you knew each other well, although, the logical part of your mind told you it wasn't so? You probably never met again, but the feeling stayed with you. Has a chance meeting, perhaps with someone you met while traveling or spending a day on the beach, left an indelible impression on you? Something that a stranger said or did in some way turned your life around? If so, you probably shared prenatal eclipse ties with that person, ties of the helpful sort. Not all such encounters are so pleasant, though they are unforgettable.

The day Lee Harvey Oswald disrupted the life of John F. Kennedy did not include a physical meeting, for as far as history knows, the two never met in person. Yet an encounter did take place on November 22, 1963, in Dallas, Texas, one that ended John Kennedy's life and changed the course of his wife's.

The horoscopes of John F. Kennedy and his wife, the former Jacqueline Bouvier (Figure 12), contain the types of karmic aspects often found in the charts of married couples.

His prenatal eclipse in 2 Aquarius 45 forms an exact oppo-

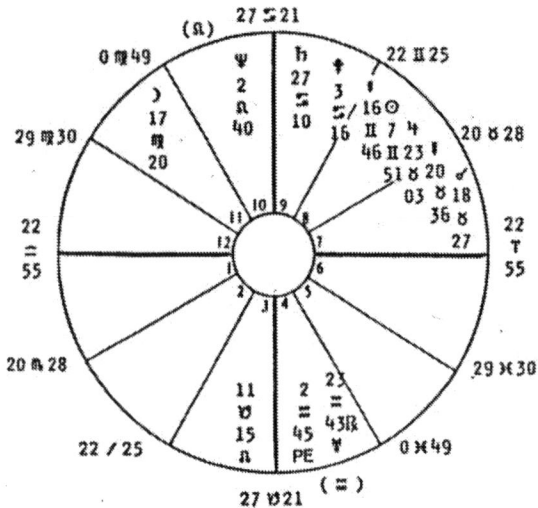

John Fitzgerald Kennedy

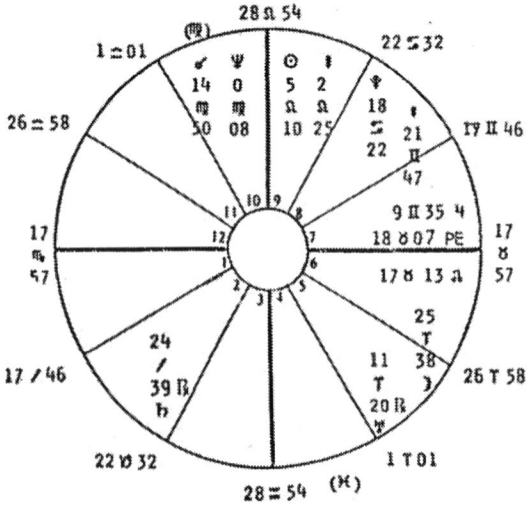

Jacqueline Kennedy Onassis

Figure 12   Karmic Ties Linking Kennedy and Oswald

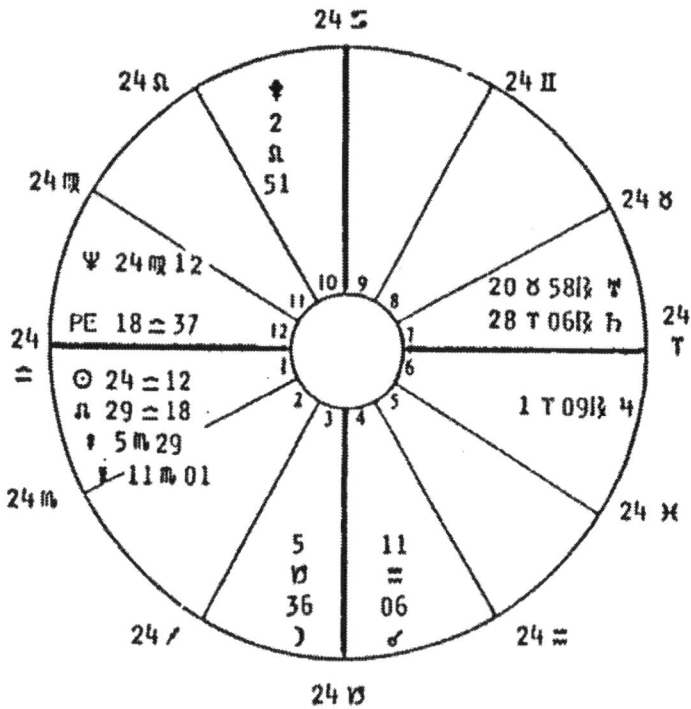

Lee Harvey Oswald

NAME	PE	RELATIONSHIP ASPECTS		
		JFK	JKO	LHO
JFK —	2≈45 —	...	♂☿	♂♅
JKO —	18ඊ07 —	△),♂♂	...	⊼PE
LHO —	18≏37 —	⊼♂	□♀,⊼PE—	...

Figure 12A   Karmic Ties Linking Kennedy and Oswald

sition with her natal Mercury. Her prenatal eclipse in 18 Taurus 07 exactly conjuncts his natal Mars, ruler of his natal seventh house placed in that house, and trines his natal Moon. Moreover, his initial eclipse in 28 Leo (9N Saros series) conjuncts her Midheaven, and her initial eclipse in 22 Libra (3N Saros series) conjuncts his Ascendant. There is little doubt that theirs was a karmic match.

Where does Lee Harvey Oswald who allegedly ended the marriage with the assassination of John Kennedy fit in? His solar chart (Figure 12) shows that his prenatal eclipse in 18 Libra 37 made an inconjunct with Jacqueline's prenatal eclipse and also exactly squared her natal Pluto, her chart ruler placed in the natal eighth house. His prenatal eclipse formed an exact inconjunct with John Kennedy's natal Mars, an aspect suggestive of a dangerous association in a pastlife. John Kennedy's Prenatal Eclipse formed an exact opposition with Oswald's natal Pluto, a planet directly associated with death. These exact hard aspects describe past difficulties which certainly were not resolved by Oswald's action. Doubtless the three were linked karmically, but the tragic ending indicates that they again will share an incarnation.

Fortunately, the majority of one-time encounters do not culminate in tragedy or violence. There are those which bring compassion into the life of the forlorn, warmth into the life of the lonely, hope into the life of the despairing.

104

Appendix

TABLE II

SOLAR AND LUNAR ECLIPSES: 1900-1999

GMT DATE	SERIES	ZODIACAL LONGITUDE	TYPE	BEGINNING POINT	NOON/ GREATEST POINT	ENDING POINT
05/28/00	10S	6°47' ♊	☉-T	117W-18N	45W-45N	32E-25N
06/13/00	10N	21°39' ♐	☽-A	--	-	-
11/22/00	11N	29°33' ♋	☉-A	3E-06S	66E-33S	135E-18S
12/06/00	11S	13°53' ♊	☽-A	--	--	-
05/03/01	11N	12°36' ♏	☽-A	--	--	-
05/18/01	11S	26°34' ♉	☉-T	40E-27S	97E-02S	157E-13S
10/27/01	12S	3°30' ♉	☽-P	--	-	-
11/11/01	12N	18°14' ♏	☉-A	13E-37N	66E-12N	122E-17N
04/08/02	12S-E*	17°48' ♈	☉-P	124W-60N	143W-72N	176E-82N
04/22/02	12N	1°42' ♏	☽-T	--	-	-
05/07/02	12S	16°25' ♉	☉-P	162E-53S	125W-70S	108W-32S
10/17/02	13S	22°56' ♈	☽-T	--	-	-
10/31/02	13N	6°59' ♏	☉-P	20E-58N	101E-71N	106E-33N
03/29/03	13S	7°11' ♈	☉-A	80E-40N	150E-65N	117W-75N
04/12/03	13N	20°56' ♎	☽-P	--	-	--
09/21/03	14N	27°01' ♍	☉-T	31E-46S	101E-70S	179E-82S
10/06/03	14S	12°11' ♈	☽-P	--	-	-
03/03/04	14N	11°07' ♍	☽-A	--	--	-
03/17/04	14S	26°13' ♓	☉-A	36E-10S	96E-06N	157E-25N
03/31/04	14N	10°23' ♎	☽-A	--	-	-
09/09/04	15N	16°42' ♍	☉-T	163E-08N	133W-05S	70W-27S
09/24/04	15S	1°14' ♈	☽-A	-	-	-
02/19/05	15N	0°29' ♍	☽-P	--	-	-
03/06/05	15S	14°59' ♓	☉-A	31E-52S	110E-43S	172E-18S
08/15/05	16S	21°37' ♎	☽-P	--	--	-
08/30/05	16N	6°28' ♍	☉-T	96W-50N	22W-45N	55E-18N
02/09/06	16N	19°40' ♌	☽-T	--	-	-
02/23/06	16S	3°48' ♓	☉-P	21W-67S	170W-72S	139E-37S
07/21/06	17N-E	27°30' ♋	☉-P	58W-51S	33W-69S	11E-60S
08/04/06	17S	11°13' ♎	☽-T	--	-	--
08/20/06	17N	26°07' ♌	☉-P	49E-72N	66E-71N	113W-47N
01/14/07	17S	22°56' ♑	☉-T	42E-50N	89E-39N	131E-57N
01/29/07	17N	8°31' ♌	☽-P	--	--	-
07/10/07	18N	17°12' ♋	☉-A	100W-34S	50W-17S	1W-37S
07/25/07	18S	1°05' ♎	☽-P	-.	--	-
01/03/08	18S	12°08' ♑	☉-T	154E-11N	145W-12S	85W-10N
01/18/08	18N	27°05' ♋	☽-A	--	-	--

GMT DATE	SERIES	ZODIACAL LONGITUDE	TYPE	BEGINNING POINT	NOON/ GREATEST POINT	ENDING POINT
06/14/08	19S	23°04' ♐	)-A	-	-	-
06/28/08	19N	6°32' ♋	☉-A	130W-05N	67W-31N	1W-10N
07/13/08	19S	21°02' ♑	)-A	-	-	-
12/07/08	19N	15°25' ♊	)-A	-	-	-
12/23/08	19S	1°17' ♑	☉-A	73W-23S	3E-53S	86E-32S
06/04/09	1S	12°46' ♐	)-T			
06/17/09	1N	26°05' ♊	☉-T	82E-50N	173W-88N	43W-60N
11/27/09	1N	4°29' ♊	)-T			
12/12/09	1S	20°11' ♐	☉-P	159E-39S	86E-65S	17W-55S
05/09/10	2N-E	17°43' ♉	☉-T	112E-73S	UNKNOWN	156E-47S
05/24/10	2S	2°10' ♐	)-T			
11/02/10	2S	8°46' ♏	☉-P	119W-63N	155E-62N	165W-18N
11/17/10	2N	23°47' ♉	)-T			
04/28/11	3N	7°30' ♉	☉-T	148E-37S	155W-01S	90W-11N
05/13/11	3S	21°22' ♏	)-A			
10/22/11	3S	27°33' ♎	☉-A	61E-45N	118E-11N	178E-08S
11/06/11	3N	13°07' ♉	)-A	-		
04/01/12	4S	11°49' ♎	)-P			
04/17/12	4N	27°05' ♈	☉-A	61W-05N	1W-46N	89E-57N
09/26/12	4N	3°00' ♈	)-P			
10/10/12	4S	16°53' ♎	☉-T	93W-04N	33W-35S	47E-52S
03/22/13	5S	1°16' ♎	)-T			
04/06/13	5N	16°19' ♈	☉-P	151W-29N	176E-61N	38E-82N
08/31/13	5S-E	7°48' ♍	☉-P	13E-78N	27W-62N	47W-44N
09/15/13	5N	22°03' ♓	)-T			
09/30/13	5S	6°25' ♎	☉-P	43E-17S	12E-61S	178E-75S
02/25/14	6N	5°33' ♓	☉-A	31W-78S	UNKNOWN	91W-43S
03/12/14	6S	20°46' ♍	)-P			
08/21/14	6S	27°35' ♌	☉-T	121W-72N	2E-71N	71E-24N
09/04/14	6N	11°11' ♓	)-P	-		
01/31/15	7S	10°14' ♌	)-A			
02/14/15	7N	24°25' ♒	☉-A	43E-36S	118E-26S	175E-13N
03/02/15	7S	10°06' ♍	)-A			
07/26/15	7N	2°25' ♒	)-A			
08/10/15	7S	17°12' ♌	☉-A	130E-23N	162W-17N	106W-22S
08/24/15	7N	00°37' ♓	)-A			
01/20/16	8S	28°58' ♋	)-P			
02/03/16	8N	13°31' ♒	☉-T	122W-07N	62W-16N	10W-49N
07/15/16	8N	22°20' ♑	)-P			
07/30/16	8S	6°34' ♌	☉-A	89E-28S	142E-36S	179E-63S
12/24/16	9N-E	2°44' ♑	☉-P	48W-67S	32W-66S	18W-64S
01/08/17	9S	17°29' ♋	)-T			
01/23/17	9N	2°45' ♒	☉-P	18E-28N	26E-63N	96E-60N
06/19/17	9S-E	27°39' ♊	☉-P	119W-53N	150E-66N	73E-46N
07/04/17	9N	12°18' ♑	)-T			
07/19/17	9S**	25°51' ♋	☉-P	94W-53S	102W-70S	129W-69S
12/14/17	10N	21°50' ♐	☉-A	88W-59S	38E-90S	155E-56S
12/28/17	10S	6°07' ♋	)-T			
06/08/18	10S	17°16' ♊	☉-T	130E-26N	152W-51N	75W-25N
06/24/18	10N	2°05' ♑	)-P			
12/03/18	11N	10°40' ♐	☉-A	119W-11S	53W-36S	15W-15S
12/17/18	11S	25°04' ♊	)-A			
05/15/19	11N	23°09' ♏	)-A			
05/29/19	11S	7°06' ♊	☉-T	75W-19S	18W-04N	42E-12S

GMT DATE	SERIES	ZODIACAL LONGITUDE	TYPE	BEGINNING POINT	NOON/ GREATEST POINT	ENDING POINT
11/07/19	12S	14°31' ♉	)-P	--	--	--
11/22/19	12N	29°17' ♏	⊙-A	103W-31N	50W-07N	4E-19N
05/03/20	12N	12°19' ♏	)-T	--	--	--
05/18/20	12S	27°00' ♉	⊙-P	46W-46S	108W-69S	133W-32S
10/27/20	13S	3°52' ♉	)-T	--	--	--
11/10/20	13N	17°58' ♏	⊙-P	96W-53N	30E-70N	15E-34N
04/08/21	13S	17°59' ♈	⊙-A	43W-45N	34E-75N	152E-77N
04/22/21	13N	1°38' ♏	)-T	--	--	--
10/01/21	14N	7°47' ♎	⊙-T	97W-52S	19W-84S	126E-86S
10/16/21	14S	23°02' ♈	)-P	--	--	--
03/13/22	14N	22°06' ♍	)-A	--	--	--
03/28/22	14S	7°04' ♈	T	76W-08S	17W-13N	47E-27N
04/11/22	14N	21°10' ♎	)-A	--	--	--
09/21/22	15N	27°24' ♍	⊙-T	43E-05N	106E-12S	173E-30S
10/01/22	15S	11°59' ♈	)-A	--	--	--
03/03/23	15N	11°32' ♍	)-P	--	--	--
03/17/23	15S	25°55' ♓	⊙-A	76W-50S	4W-36S	57E-15S
08/26/23	16S	2°09' ♓	)-P	--	--	--
09/10/23	16N	17°06' ♍	⊙-T	154E-48N	128W-38N	64W-14N
02/20/24	16N	00°46' ♍	)-T	--	--	--
03/05/24	16S	14°49' ♓	⊙-P	131E-68S	56W-72S	14W-35S
07/31/24	17N-E	8°16' ♌	⊙-P	164E-55S	146E-70S	100E-68S
08/14/24	17S	21°43' ♒	)-T	--	--	--
08/30/24	17N	6°40' ♍	⊙-P	42E-72N	73E-72N	129W-41N
01/24/25	17S	4°08' ♒	⊙-T	95W-48N	44W-42N	3W-61N
02/08/25	17N	19°39' ♌	)-P	--	--	--
07/20/25	18N	27°37' ♋	⊙-A	162E-37S	148W-26S	100W-47S
08/04/25	18S	11°34' ♒	)-P	--	--	--
01/14/26	18S	23°21' ♑	⊙-T	21E-07N	82E-10S	142E-14N
01/28/26	18N	8°14' ♌	)-A	--	--	--
06/25/26	19S	3°31' ♑	)-A	--	--	--
07/09/26	19N	16°37' ♋	⊙-A	132E-04N	165W-25N	104W-01N
07/25/26	19S	1°30' ♒	)-A	--	--	--
12/19/26	19N	26°35' ♊	)-A	--	--	--
01/03/27	19S	12°29' ♑	⊙-A	156E-27S	125W-52S	46W-27S
06/15/27	1S	23°14' ♐	)-T	--	--	--
06/29/27	1N	6°31' ♋	⊙-T	16W-46N	84E-78N	169W-51N
12/08/27	1N	15°38' ♊	)-T	--	--	--
12/24/27	1S	1°21' ♑	⊙-P	34W-43S	48E-66S	145E-51S
05/19/28	2N-E	28°17' ♉	⊙-T	12E-67S	22E-63S	29E-58S
06/03/28	2S	12°39' ♐	)-T	--	--	--
06/17/28	2N**	26°22' ♊	⊙-P	96E-62N	71E-66N	42E-67N
11/12/28	2S	19°46' ♏	⊙-P	6E-60N	81E-63N	78E-21N
11/27/28	2N	4°54' ♊	)-T	--	--	--
05/09/29	3N	18°07' ♉	⊙-T	35E-37S	89E-01S	153E-05N
05/23/29	3S	1°53' ♐	)-A	--	--	--
11/01/29	3S	8°35' ♏	⊙-A	55W-43N	1W-09N	59E-04S
11/17/29	3N	24°10' ♉	)-A	--	--	--
04/13/30	4S	22°35' ♎	)-P	--	--	--
04/28/30	4N	7°45' ♉	⊙-A	173W-03N	113W-45N	23W-50N
10/07/30	4N	13°47' ♈	)-P	--	--	--
10/21/30	4S	27°46' ♎	⊙-T	146E-04N	155W-36S	72W-41S

GMT DATE	SERIES	ZODIACAL LONGITUDE	TYPE	BEGINNING POINT	NOON/ GREATEST POINT	ENDING POINT
04/02/31	5S	12°07' ♎	☽-T	--	--	--
04/18/31	5N	27°03' ♈	☉-P	100W-27N	59W-62N	80E-76N
09/12/31	5S-E*	18°27' ♍	☉-P	140E-71N	153E-61N	162E-51N
09/26/31	5N	2°45' ♈	☽-T	--	--	--
10/11/31	5S	17°15' ♎	☉-P	80E-16S	120E-61S	65W-71S
03/07/32	6N	16°32' ♓	☉-A	179W-75S	UNKNOWN	152E-47S
03/22/32	6S	1°41' ♎	☽-P	--	--	--
08/31/32	6S	8°10' ♍	☉-T	109E-80N	109W-79N	41W-28N
09/14/32	6N	21°49' ♓	☽-P	--	--	--
02/10/33	7S	21°22' ♌	☽-A	--	--	--
02/24/33	7N	5°29' ♓	☉-A	70W-39S	5W-24S	42E-14N
03/12/33	7S	21°05' ♍	☽-A	--	--	--
08/05/33	7N	12°53' ♒	☽-A	--	--	--
08/21/33	7S	27°42' ♌	☉-A	24E-30N	94E-18N	150E-20S
09/04/33	7N	11°12' ♓	☽-A	--	--	--
01/30/34	8S	10°07' ♌	☽-P	--	--	--
02/14/34	8N	24°39' ♒	☉-T	108E-04N	168E-19N	137W-52N
07/26/34	8N	2°48' ♒	☽-P	--	--	--
08/10/34	8S	17°02' ♌	☉-A	11W-19S	43E-33S	88E-62S
01/05/35	9N-E*	13°57' ♑	☉-P	106E-65S	110E-65S	114E-65S
01/19/35	9S	28°39' ♋	☽-T	--	--	--
02/03/35	9N	13°56' ♒	☉-P	116W-25N	115W-63N	36W-65N
06/30/35	9S-E*	8°04' ♋	☉-P	130W-60N	39W-65N	23E-47N
07/16/35	9N	22°45' ♑	☽-T	--	--	--
07/30/35	9S	6°18' ♌	☉-P	10W-43S	6E-63S	36E-71S
12/25/35	10N	3°01' ♑	☉-A	135E-62S	93E-88S	25E-53S
01/08/36	10S	17°19' ♋	☽-T	--	--	--
06/19/36	10S	27°44' ♊	☉-T	16E-34N	101E-56N	179E-26N
07/04/36	10N	12°31' ♑	☽-P	--	--	--
12/13/36	11N	21°49' ♐	☉-A	118E-15S	173W-38S	107W-11S
12/28/36	11S	6°16' ♋	☽-A	--	--	--
05/25/37	11N	3°40' ♐	☽-A	--	--	--
06/08/37	11S	17°36' ♊	☉-T	169E-12S	131W-10N	71W-12S
11/18/37	12S	25°35' ♉	☽-P	--	--	--
12/02/37	12N	10°23' ♐	☉-A	139E-26N	169W-04N	115W-22N
05/14/38	12N	22°54' ♏	☽-T	--	--	--
05/29/38	12S	7°32' ♊	☉-T	52W-65S	27W-52S	10E-61S
11/07/38	13S	14°51' ♉	☽-T	--	--	--
11/22/38	13N	29°02' ♏	☉-P	144W-48N	162E-69N	138E-36N
04/19/39	13S	28°44' ♈	☉-A	167W-54N	79W-88N	76E-78N
05/03/39	13N	12°18' ♏	☽-T	--	--	--
10/12/39	14N	18°37' ♎	☉-T	130E-60S	UNKNOWN	72E-82S
10/28/39	14S	3°57' ♉	☽-P	--	--	--
03/23/40	14N	3°01' ♎	☽-A	--	--	--
04/07/40	14S	17°52' ♈	☉-A	174W-04S	127W-20N	60W-29N
04/22/40	14N	1°54' ♏	☽-A	--	--	--
10/01/40	15N	8°11' ♎	☉-T	79W-03N	16W-19S	54E-33S
10/16/40	15S	22°49' ♈	☽-A	--	--	--
03/13/41	15N	22°31' ♍	☽-P	--	--	--
03/27/41	15S	7°46' ♈	☉-A	178E-47S	116W-29S	57W-12S
09/05/41	16S	12°45' ♓	☽-P	--	--	--
09/21/41	16N	27°48' ♍	☉-T	42E-45N	114E-30N	177E-10N
03/03/42	16N	11°48' ♍	☽-T	--	--	--
03/16/42	16S	25°46' ♓	☉-P	22E-68S	77E-72S	109E-32S

108

GMT DATE	SERIES	ZODIACAL LONGITUDE	TYPE	BEGINNING POINT	NOON/ GREATEST POINT	ENDING POINT
08/12/42	17N-E*	18°45' ♌	⊙-P	90E-62S	100E-70S	127E-75S
08/26/42	17S	2°17' ♓	)-T	-	-	-
09/10/42	17N	17°18' ♍	⊙-P	135E-71N	50W-72N	13W-37N
02/04/43	17S	15°17' ♒	⊙-T	129E-47N	176W-47N	136W-66N
02/20/43	17N	00°43' ♍	)-P	-	-	-
08/01/43	18N	8°03' ♌	⊙-A	62E-42S	114E-37S	159E-58S
08/15/43	18S	22°05' ♒	)-P	-	-	-
01/25/44	18S	4°33' ♒	⊙-T	112W-03N	49W-07S	9E-19N
02/09/44	18N	19°21' ♌	)-A	-	-	-
07/06/44	19S	13°58' ♑	)-A	-	-	-
07/20/44	19N	27°22' ♋	⊙-A	33E-03N	95E-19N	154E-07S
08/04/44	19S	11°59' ♒	)-A	-	-	-
12/29/44	19N	7°47' ♋	)-A	-	-	-
01/14/45	19S	23°41' ♑	⊙-A	27E-31S	108E-51S	177W-23S
06/25/45	1S	3°40' ♑	)-P	-	-	-
07/09/45	1N	16°57' ♋	⊙-T	116W-44N	20W-70N	72E-41N
12/19/45	1N	26°50' ♊	)-T	-	-	-
01/03/46	1S	12°33' ♑	⊙-P	92E-47S	178W-67S	87W-47S
05/30/46	2N-E	8°49' ♊	⊙-P	166W-53S	101W-64S	86W-28S
06/14/46	2S	23°05' ♐	)-T	-	-	-
06/29/46	2N	6°49' ♋	⊙-P	3E-58N	51E-67N	109E-61N
11/23/46	2S	00°50' ♐	⊙-P	11W-56N	45W-63N	41W-25N
12/08/46	2N	16°03' ♊	)-T	-	-	-
05/20/47	3N	28°42' ♉	⊙-T	78W-36S	25W-02S	37E-02S
06/03/47	3S	12°22' ♐	)-P	-	-	-
11/12/47	3S	19°36' ♏	⊙-A	173W-41N	121W-06N	62W-01N
11/28/47	3N	5°16' ♊	)-A	-	-	-
04/23/48	4S	3°18' ♏	)-P	-	-	-
05/09/48	4N	18°22' ♉	⊙-A	77E-02N	138E-44N	136W-43N
10/18/48	4N	24°37' ♈	)-A	-	-	-
11/01/48	4S	8°44' ♏	⊙-T	22E-04N	82E-37S	165W-43S
04/13/49	5S	22°54' ♎	)-T	-	-	-
04/28/49	5N	7°42' ♉	⊙-P	5E-25N	56E-62N	166W-70N
10/07/49	5N	13°30' ♈	)-T	-	-	-
10/21/49	5S	28°09' ♎	⊙-P	154W-15S	107W-62S	56E-66S
03/18/50	6N	27°28' ♓	⊙-A	48E-72S	41E-61S	35E-50S
04/02/50	6S	12°32' ♎	)-T	-	-	-
09/12/50	6S	18°43' ♍	⊙-T	67W-85N	175W-47N	155E-34N
09/26/50	6N	2°31' ♈	)-T	-	-	-
02/21/51	7S	2°26' ♍	)-A	-	-	-
03/07/51	7N	16°29' ♓	⊙-A	161E-42S	127W-21S	69W-14N
03/23/51	7S	2°00' ♎	)-A	-	-	-
08/17/51	7N	23°25' ♒	)-A	-	-	-
09/01/51	7S	8°16' ♍	⊙-A	81W-36N	11W-19N	46E-18S
09/15/51	7N	21°52' ♓	)-A	-	-	-
02/11/52	8S	21°14' ♌	)-P	-	-	-
02/25/52	8N	5°43' ♓	⊙-T	21W-01N	39E-22N	99E-54N
08/05/52	8N	13°17' ♒	)-P	-	-	-
08/20/52	8S	27°31' ♌	⊙-A	112W-11S	56W-30S	4W-61S
01/29/53	9S	9°48' ♌	)-T	-	-	-
02/14/53	9N	25°03' ♒	⊙-P	111W-22N	105W-62N	164E-68N
07/11/53	9S-E	18°30' ♋	⊙-P	1E-66N	71E-64N	118E-49N
07/26/53	9N	3°12' ♒	)-T	-	-	-
08/09/53	9S	16°45' ♌	⊙-P	113E-35S	115E-62S	55W-73S

GMT DATE	SERIES	ZODIACAL LONGITUDE	TYPE	BEGINNING POINT	NOON/ GREATEST POINT	ENDING POINT
01/05/54	10N	14°13' ♑	⊙-A	3W-66S	31W-85S	106W-51S
01/19/54	10S	28°30' ♋	)-T	-	-	-
06/30/54	10S	8°10' ♋	⊙-T	99W-42N	5W-62N	74E-26N
07/16/54	10N	22°57' ♑	)-P	-	-	-
12/25/54	11N	2°59' ♑	⊙-A	5W-20S	67E-39S	131E-07S
01/08/55	11S	17°28' ♋	)-A	-	-	-
06/05/55	11N	14°08' ♐	)-A	-	-	-
06/20/55	11S	28°05' ♊	⊙-T	55E-04S	117E-15N	177E-12S
11/29/55	12S	6°42' ♊	)-P	-	-	-
12/14/55	12N	21°31' ♐	⊙-A	19E-21N	72E-02N	124E-25N
05/24/56	12N	3°25' ♐	)-P	-	-	-
06/08/56	12S	18°02' ♊	⊙-T	178E-55S	141W-40S	100W-55S
11/18/56	13S	25°55' ♉	)-T	-	-	-
12/02/56	13N	10°09' ♐	⊙-P	21W-43N	65W-68N	97W-38N
04/29/57	13S	9°23' ♉	⊙-T	57E-66N	40E-71N	17E-74N
05/13/57	13N	22°52' ♏	)-T	-	-	-
10/23/57	14N	29°31' ♎	⊙-P	19W-70S	23W-71S	28W-73S
11/07/57	14S	14°55' ♉	)-T	-	-	-
04/04/58	14N	13°52' ♎	)-A	-	-	-
04/19/58	14S	28°34' ♈	⊙-A	66E-01N	126E-28N	164W-31N
05/03/58	14N	12°34' ♏	)-P	-	-	-
10/12/58	15N	19°01' ♎	⊙-T	157E-01S	139W-26S	67W-34S
10/27/58	15S	3°43' ♉	)-A	-	-	-
03/24/59	15N	3°26' ♎	)-P	-	-	-
04/08/59	15S	17°34' ♈	⊙-A	72E-43S	133E-21S	168W-10S
09/17/59	16S	23°24' ♓	)-A	-	-	-
10/02/59	16N	8°34' ♎	⊙-T	72W-42N	6W-23N	56E-07N
03/13/60	16N	22°47' ♍	)-T	-	-	-
03/27/60	16S	6°39' ♈	⊙-P	15W-66S	152W-72S	129W-30S
09/05/60	17S	12°53' ♓	)-T	-	-	-
09/20/60	17N	27°58' ♍	⊙-P	129W-69N	74E-72N	104E-33N
02/15/61	17S	26°25' ♒	⊙-T	6W-46N	53E-53N	94E-72N
03/02/61	17N	11°45' ♍	)-P	-	-	-
08/11/61	18N	18°31' ♌	⊙-A	39W-48S	14E-50S	51E-69S
08/26/61	18S	2°39' ♓	)-T	-	-	-
02/05/62	18S	15°43' ♒	⊙-T	116E-01N	179E-04S	122W-23N
02/19/62	18N	00°25' ♍	)-A	-	-	-
07/17/62	19S	24°25' ♑	)-A	-	-	-
07/31/62	19N	7°49' ♌	⊙-A	67W-02N	5W-12N	51E-15S
08/15/62	19S	22°30' ♒	)-A	-	-	-
01/09/63	19N	18°59' ♋	)-A	-	-	-
01/25/63	19S	4°52' ♒	⊙-A	102W-35S	19W-49S	52E-20S
07/06/63	1S	14°06' ♑	)-P	-	-	-
07/20/63	1N	27°24' ♋	⊙-T	143E-43N	126W-62N	44W-33N
12/30/63	1N	8°01' ♋	)-T	-	-	-
01/14/64	1S	23°43' ♑	⊙-P	144W-51S	43W-68S	41E-44S
06/10/64	2N-E	19°19' ♊	⊙-P	80W-52S	136W-65S	158W-35S
06/25/64	2S	3°30' ♑	)-T	-	-	-
07/09/64	2N	17°16' ♋	⊙-P	99W-57N	173W-68N	118E-54N
12/04/64	2S	11°56' ♐	⊙-P	129E-52N	174W-64N	162W-30N
12/19/64	2N	27°14' ♊	)-T	-	-	-
05/30/65	3N	9°13' ♊	⊙-T	171E-36S	137W-04S	78W-10S
06/14/65	3S	22°48' ♐	)-P	-	-	-
11/23/65	3S	00°40' ♐	⊙-A	65E-38N	116E-04N	175E-05N
12/08/65	3N	16°25' ♊	)-A	-	-	-

GMT DATE	SERIES	ZODIACAL LONGITUDE	TYPE	BEGINNING POINT	NOON/GREATEST POINT	ENDING POINT
05/04/66	4S	13°56' ♏	)-A	–	–	–
05/20/66	4N	28°55' ♉	☉-A	30W-02N	31E-41N	113E-36N
10/29/66	4N	5°32' ♉	)-A	–	–	–
11/12/66	4S	19°45' ♏	☉-T	104W-02N	43W-38S	40E-38S
04/24/67	5S	3°37' ♏	)-T	–	–	–
05/09/67	5N	18°18' ♉	☉-P	108E-24N	169E-65N	55E-63N
10/18/67	5N	24°21' ♈	)-T	–	–	–
11/02/67	5S	9°07' ♏	☉-T	19W-56S	28W-62S	40W-67S
03/28/68	6N	8°19' ♈	☉-P	146W-72S	80E-61S	109E-13S
04/13/68	6S	23°23' ♎	)-T	–	–	–
09/22/68	6S	29°30' ♍	☉-T	49W-67N	98E-61N	66E-09N
10/06/68	6N	13°17' ♈	)-T	–	–	–
03/18/69	7N	27°25' ♓	☉-A	44E-45S	112E-19S	172W-13N
04/02/69	7S	12°51' ♎	)-A	–	–	–
08/27/69	7N	3°58' ♓	)-A	–	–	–
09/11/69	7S	18°53' ♍	☉-A	173E-41N	117E-19N	60W-16S
09/25/69	7N	2°35' ♈	)-A	–	–	–
02/21/70	8S	2°18' ♍	)-P	–	–	–
03/07/70	8N	16°44' ♓	☉-T	149W-02S	88W-25N	23W-55N
08/17/70	8N	23°49' ♎	)-P	–	–	–
08/31/70	8S	8°04' ♍	☉-A	147E-05S	157W-29S	98W-59S
09/15/70	8N	22°12' ♓	)-A	–	–	–
02/10/71	9S	20°55' ♌	)-T	–	–	–
02/25/71	9N	6°09' ♓	☉-P	21E-19N	34E-62N	72W-72N
07/22/71	9S-E*	28°56' ♋	☉-P	144E-69N	177W-64N	150W-54N
08/06/71	9N	13°41' ♒	)-T	–	–	–
08/20/71	9S	27°15' ♌	☉-P	144W-28S	135W-62S	146E-74S
01/16/72	10N	25°25' ♑	☉-A	143W-69S	156W-81S	123E-49S
01/30/72	10S	9°39' ♌	)-T	–	–	–
07/10/72	10S	18°37' ♋	☉-T	144E-51N	111W-67N	31W-28N
07/26/72	10N	3°24' ♒	)-P	–	–	–
01/04/73	11N	14°10' ♑	☉-A	128W-25S	54W-40S	8E-08S
01/18/73	11S	28°40' ♋	)-A	–	–	–
06/15/73	11N	24°35' ♐	)-A	–	–	–
06/30/73	11S	8°32' ♋	☉-T	60W-05N	6E-19N	65E-13S
07/15/73	11N	22°51' ♑	)-A	–	–	–
12/10/73	12S	17°51' ♊	)-P	–	–	–
12/24/73	12N	2°40' ♑	☉-A	102W-16N	47W-01N	3E-29N
06/04/74	12N	13°54' ♐	)-P	–	–	–
06/20/74	12S	28°30' ♊	☉-T	59E-45S	106E-33S	148E-53S
11/29/74	13S	7°01' ♊	)-T	–	–	–
12/13/74	13N	21°17' ♐	☉-P	103W-38N	70W-67N	29W-41N
05/11/75	13S	19°59' ♉	☉-P	00-32N	81W-70N	150E-50N
05/25/75	13N	3°25' ♐	)-T	–	–	–
11/03/75	14N	10°29' ♏	☉-P	91W-28S	162W-71S	57E-52S
11/18/75	14S	25°58' ♉	)-T	–	–	–
04/29/76	14S	9°13' ♉	☉-A	41W-07N	21E-35N	95E-32N
05/13/76	14N	23°10' ♏	)-P	–	–	–
10/23/76	15N	29°55' ♎	☉-T	31E-04S	95E-31S	171E-33S
11/06/76	15S	14°41' ♉	)-A	–	–	–
04/04/77	15N	14°17' ♎	)-P	–	–	–
04/18/77	15S	28°17' ♈	☉-A	33W-38S	25E-14S	83E-08S

GMT DATE	SERIES	ZODIACAL LONGITUDE	TYPE	BEGINNING POINT	NOON/ GREATEST POINT	ENDING POINT
09/27/77	16S	4°07' ♈	)-A	-	-	-
10/12/77	16N	19°24' ♎	☉-T	170E-39N	127W-16N	66W-06N
03/24/78	16N	3°40' ♎	)-T	-	-	-
04/07/78	16S	17°27' ♈	☉-P	92W-62S	23E-72S	10E-29S
09/16/78	17S	23°33' ♓	)-T	-	-	-
10/02/78	17N	8°43' ♎	☉-P	27E-66N	159E-72N	140E-31N
02/26/79	17S	7°29' ♓	☉-T	140W-47N	77W-61N	34W-77N
03/13/79	17N	22°42' ♍	)-P	-	-	-
08/22/79	18N	29°01' ♌	☉-T	142W-58S	87W-76S	87W-78S
09/06/79	18S	13°16' ♓	)-T	-	-	-
02/16/80	18S	26°50' ♒	☉-T	15W-01S	49E-01N	108E-27N
03/01/80	18N	11°26' ♍	)-A	-	-	-
07/27/80	19S	4°52' ♒	)-A	-	-	-
08/10/80	19N	18°17' ♌	☉-A	169W-01N	108W-04N	52W-23S
08/26/80	19S	3°03' ♓	)-A	-	-	-
01/20/81	19N	00°10' ♌	)-A	-	-	-
02/04/81	19S	16°02' ♒	☉-A	132E-39S	146W-46S	78W-17S
07/17/81	1S	24°31' ♑	)-P	-	-	-
07/31/81	1N	7°51' ♌	☉-T	40E-42N	128E-55N	158W-25N
01/09/82	1N	19°14' ♋	)-T	-	-	-
01/25/82	1S	4°54' ♒	☉-P	21E-55S	92W-69S	168W-41S
06/21/82	2N-E	29°47' ♊	☉-P	34W-51S	13E-66S	42E-42S
07/06/82	2S	13°55' ♑	)-T	-	-	-
07/20/82	2N	27°43' ♋	☉-P	157E-57N	64E-69N	7W-47N
12/15/82	2S	23°04' ♐	☉-P	7E-49N	57E-65N	77E-34N
12/30/82	2N	8°27' ♋	)-T	-	-	-
06/11/83	3N	19°43' ♊	☉-T	60E-36S	111E-07S	168E-18S
06/25/83	3S	3°14' ♑	)-P	-	-	-
12/04/83	3S	11°47' ♐	☉-A	58W-34S	7W-02N	50E-10N
12/20/83	3N	27°36' ♊	)-A	-	-	-
05/15/84	4S	24°31' ♏	)-A	-	-	-
05/30/84	4N	9°26' ♊	☉-A	136W-02N	74W-39N	4E-28N
06/13/84	4S	22°45' ♐	)-A	-	-	-
11/08/84	4N	16°30' ♉	)-A	-	-	-
11/22/84	4S	00°50' ♐	☉-T	128E-01S	169W-40S	88W-33S
05/04/85	5S	14°17' ♏	)-T	-	-	-
05/19/85	5N	28°50' ♉	☉-P	151E-23N	81E-63N	54W-56N
10/28/85	5N	5°15' ♉	)-T	-	-	-
11/12/85	5S	20°09' ♏	☉-T	148W-54S	165W-63S	169E-70S
04/09/86	6N	19°06' ♈	☉-P	50E-70S	161E-61S	140E-16S
04/24/86	6S	4°03' ♏	)-T	-	-	-
10/03/86	6S	10°16' ♎	☉-T	26W-66N	32W-60N	28W-56N
10/17/86	6N	24°07' ♈	)-T	-	-	-
03/29/87	7N	8°18' ♈	☉-A	71W-47S	6W-17S	54E-11N
04/14/87	7S	23°38' ♎	)-A	-	-	-
09/23/87	7S	29°34' ♍	☉-A	68E-46N	135E-19N	167W-13S
10/07/87	7N	13°22' ♈	)-P	-	-	-
03/03/88	8S	13°18' ♍	)-P	-	-	-
03/18/88	8N	27°42' ♓	☉-T	86E-04S	146E-28N	142W-54N
08/27/88	8N	4°23' ♓	)-P	-	-	-
09/11/88	8S	18°40' ♍	☉-A	44W-01N	101E-28S	165E-57S
02/20/89	9S	1°59' ♍	)-T	-	-	-
03/07/89	9N	17°10' ♓	☉-P	150W-17N	170W-61N	44W-73N
08/17/89	9N	24°12' ♎	)-T	-	-	-
08/31/89	9S	7°48' ♍	☉-P	40E-22S	123E-61S	124E-75S

GMT DATE	SERIES	ZODIACAL LONGITUDE	TYPE	BEGINNING POINT	NOON/ GREATEST POINT	ENDING POINT
01/26/90	10N	6°35' ≈	☉-A	74E-71S	22W-63S	7W-48S
02/09/90	10S	20°47' ♌	☽-T	--	--	--
07/22/90	10S	29°04' ♋	☉-T	24E-60N	142E-73N	139W-30N
08/06/90	10N	13°52' ≈	☽-P	--	--	--
01/15/91	11N	25°20' ♑	☉-A	110E-30S	170W-36S	115W-01N
01/30/91	11S	9°51' ♌	☽-A	--	--	--
06/27/91	11N	5°00' ♑	☽-A	--	--	--
07/11/91	11S	18°59' ♋	☉-T	174W-13N	105W-22N	46W-13S
07/26/91	11N	3°16' ≈	☽-A	--	--	--
12/21/91	12S	29°03' ♊	☽-P	--	--	--
01/04/92	12N	13°51' ♑	☉-A	138E-11N	170W-01N	119W-33N
06/15/92	12N	24°20' ♐	☽-P	--	--	--
06/30/92	12S	8°57' ♋	☉-T	56W-35S	9W-25S	38E-51S
12/09/92	13S	18°10' ♊	☽-T	--	--	--
12/24/92	13N	2°28' ♑	☉-P	135E-40N	168E-65N	135W-38N
05/21/93	13S	00°31' ♊	☉-P	120W-24N	135E-66N	60E-52N
06/04/93	13N	13°55' ♐	☽-T	--	--	--
11/13/93	14N	21°32' ♏	☉-P	125E-25S	155W-65S	70W-28S
11/29/93	14S	7°03' ♊	☽-T	--	--	--
05/10/94	14S	19°48' ♉	☉-A	146W-13N	86W-40N	5W-32N
05/25/94	14N	3°43' ♐	☽-P	--	--	--
11/03/94	15N	10°54' ♏	☉-T	97W-08S	34W-35S	47E-32S
11/18/94	15S	25°42' ♉	☽-A	--	--	--
04/15/95	15N	25°04' ♎	☽-P	--	--	--
04/29/95	15S	8°56' ♉	☉-A	137W-32S	80W-05S	23W-07S
10/08/95	16S	14°54' ♈	☽-A	--	--	--
10/24/95	16N	00°18' ♏	☉-T	51E-35N	113E-08N	172E-06N
04/04/96	16N	14°31' ♎	☽-T	--	--	--
04/17/96	16S	28°12' ♈	☉-P	150E-55S	175W-30S	135W-22S
09/27/96	17S	4°17' ♈	☽-T	--	--	--
10/12/96	17N	19°32' ♎	☉-P	90W-58N	35W-25N	50E-20N
03/09/97	17S	18°31' ♓	☉-T	89E-49N	131E-58N	165W-82N
03/24/97	17N	3°35' ♎	☽-P	--	--	--
09/01/97	18N	9°34' ♍	☉-P	115E-30S	170E-45S	105W-60S
09/16/97	18S	23°56' ♓	☽-T	--	--	--
02/26/98	18S	7°55' ♓	☉-T	144W-02S	80W-05N	19W-30N
03/13/98	18N	22°24' ♍	☽-A	--	--	--
08/08/98	19S	15°21' ≈	☽-A	--	--	--
08/22/98	19N	28°48' ♌	☉-A	87W-01S	145E-03S	155W-29S
09/06/98	19S	13°40' ♓	☽-A	--	--	--
01/31/99	19N	11°20' ♌	☽-A	--	--	--
02/16/99	19S	27°08' ≈	☉-A	8E-42S	92E-40S	154E-14S
07/28/99	1S	4°58' ≈	☽-P	--	--	--
08/11/99	1N	18°21' ♌	☉-T	65W-41N	23E-45N	87E-17N

*Final eclipse in series.   **Initial eclipse in series.
Key: N=North; S=South; E=East or, in the SERIES column, the earlier starting
of two concurrently members of the same series; W=West; A=lunar appulse or
annular solar eclipse; P=partial eclipse; T=total eclipse.

Note: Geographical positions for eclipses, given to the nearest degree,
do not describe the complete path of an eclipse, just those points
pertinent to the Prenatal Eclipse.

Bibliography

American Ephemeris and Nautical Almanac, 1910-1975. Nautical Almanac Office, U.S. Naval Observatory.

Arizona State University Government Documents 965-3387. U.S. Government Printing Office. Washington, D.C.

Astronomical Phenomena, 1983-1985. Nautical Almanac Office, U.S. Naval Observatory. Espanek, Fred.

Fifty Year Canon of Solar Eclipses: 1986-2035. Cambridge, MA: Sky Publishing, 1987.

Garrett, Helen Adams. *The Karmic Horoscope*. Tempe, AZ: AFA, 2002.

Garrett, Helen and Jim. *Karma by Declinations*. Tempe, AZ: AFA, 2002.

Lineman, Rose. *Eclipses: Astrological Guideposts*. Tempe, AZ: AFA, 1984.

Lineman, Rose. *Eclipse Interpretation Manual*. Tempe, AZ: AFA, 1986.

Lineman, Rose. "Prenatal Eclipse," *Today's Astrologer*, American Federation of Astrologers bulletin, Vol. 51, No. 7 (July 1989), pp. 227-232.

Lineman, Rose and Popelka, Jan. *Compendium of Astrology*. Gloucester, MA: Para Research. 1984.

Mundane Data, Lunations and Eclipses. Tempe, AZ: AFA.

Oppolzer, Theodor von. *Canon of Eclipses*, trans. 0. Gingerich. Reprinted 1962. New York, NY: Dover Publications.

World Almanac, 1923-1973. New York, NY: Scripps Howard Co.

9 780866 904155